Sportin' House

Other Books
by Stephen Longstreet

Sportin' House

A History of the New Orleans Sinners and the Birth of Jazz

Text and Pictures

by

Stephen Longstreet

Rich gal she rides in a big Cadillac.
Poor gal she drives a Model A.
My gal she only has to wave her thumb,
And she gets there right away . . .

SHERBOURNE PRESS, INC.
LOS ANGELES, CALIFORNIA

Table of Contents

This book contains nothing but Facts, and is of the greatest value to strangers when in this part of the city. The names of the residents will be found in this Directory, alphabetically arranged, under the headings "White" and "Colored," from alpha to omega. The names in capitals are landladies only.

You will find the boundary of the Tenderloin District, or Storyville: North side Iberville Street to south side St. Louis, and east side North Basin to west side North Robertson Street.

This is the boundary in which the women are compelled to live, according to law.

From The Blue Book, the 1902 Directory and Guide of the New Orleans Sporting District

Chicken today,
Feathers tomorrow.
                    Sporting House proverb

How this book came to be

For over thirty years this writer and painter has been probing the world of the jazz man, his background, his roots, and his destiny. Between other projects I have always gone back to the subject with colors and paper, tape recorder and often just the price of a bottle of gin, to see, hear, sketch, and gossip with the neglected survivors of the only truly home-grown American art form.

It has resulted in a vast piling up of material, out of which came two definitive histories, *The Real Jazz Old and New*, Louisiana State University Press, 1956, and *Encyclopedie du Jazz*, Somegy Grund, 1958, also published in German as *Knaurs Jazz Lexikon*, in Spanish as *Enciclopedia del Jazz*, and in Italian as *Dizionario del Jazz*.

The jazz paintings and drawings done by the author have been exhibited internationally in galleries and museums, and many are now in private hands. The biggest collection is at Yale University, and there are others at the University of California at Los Angeles and Boston University, where a Stephen Longstreet collection of books, original manuscripts, and works of art is housed by the director, Howard B. Gottlieb. There is also a group in the New Orleans Jazz Museum.

This book is the result of certain facets of my work in the field coming into historical focus; only a few unhistoric, over-sensational texts have touched on the dissolute subject of the sporting houses of New Orleans and their part in the birth of jazz. It is a bawdy story and sometimes not in the best of taste, but history is not always polite, nor well laundered and *l'homme moyen sensual* is often the part of the past that interests us.

> *Rufus Akes and Rastus Payne;*
> *They got married down in Gaines.*
> *Now they say them woods*
> *Is full of Akes and Paynes.*

My major objective has been to try and find out how jazz came about, who was there, how they played it and lived it, and what became of it. The heroes and their women may not all be housebroken, but their groans, their laments, their pleasurings and ecstasies, all helped bring about a new kind of music to the American scene. The sporting house, often called Liberty Hall, as part of the native scene looms large in our mythology, raucous and usually not written down. It may have changed its name, but the habits of its inhabitants and practitioners are classical, unchanging, always in demand. To the puritan-plagued, guilt-ridden American of the past it had a scarlet core of fascination; whispered about, sung about, leered at, it haunted the minds and memories of many respectable citizens of the Republic. For those who once visited the velvet, plush-draped parlor, bought a drink for the madame and the girls, and heard the Professor try out "Peephole Blues" on the eighty-eight keys of the Ivory floor of the whorehouse piano, the sense of sin was, in those days, an added pleasure.

When I began my research into the sources of the stone age jazz, at first often spelled *jass*, the survivors of both the sporting houses and the music, those active at the turn of the century, were still around. I sketched them, painted them, took down their words, listened to their histories, taped some of their memories. Few are now left, and I have brought back here their images and their activities as documents of two unrespected professions.

This book is based mostly on personal research, but for that part which is from the older past, I have gone to the actual sources, thin as they are, rather than to popular histories. In the early 1930's I acquired the unpublished manuscript of Nell Kimball, who, under another name, had been the madame of a New Orleans sporting house from the eighties of the last century till the brothel district called Storyville was closed in 1917. In telling the story of her life and of her business activities she was utterly and blandly frank; she had a keen eye for detail—and for a dollar—even if a weakness in spelling. Her manuscript is the most accurate close-up picture of native vice combined with music that I have found—the very scent of body powder, bourbon, and fresh linen is in it. I have used sections of it in this book to flesh out (no pun intended) the not-too-secret history of the city first called Nouvelle Orleans, and the section still known as the Vieux Carré.

I have been able to salvage some incomplete collections of three publications issued for the sporting house trade and their clients. The weekly *Mascot*, the weekly *Sunday Sun*, and the yearly guide to the Quarter, *The Blue Book*, with advertisements by the houses and the proud madames, illustrated with images of some of the inmates and the glorious over-ripe interiors of Victorian-Roman decor. This last was very likely the most exotic, erotic public guide to copulation ever produced and circulated in America. I have also hunted in the back files of old newspapers; the *New Orleans Times*, the *Picayune*, the *States*, and the *Times-Picayune*.

The sketches and drawings that illustrate this text claim as their only merit that they were done from life, and are not studio products or works of the imagination. They try to capture directly the taste, feel, and color of the places, people, and music. They attempt to recapture an era, an art, and certain places and certain people, not perhaps as God made them but as conditions and they themselves molded their destinies.

How they presented themselves to the call of, "Company, girls!" or to the cue of: "Play something nice and jazzy, professor."

It was Countess Willie V. Piazza—she ran a house of prostitution at 315 Basin Street—who put the period to the end of an era when she said, in the most edited of her remarks on the failure of the professionals to survive, "It's the goddamn country club girls giving it away for free who are ruining the business."

S. L.

BOOK ONE

THE DELTA

River boats

Chapter 1

Early to bed and early to rise;
And your girl goes out with other guys.
Lord, Lord, got those Brown's Ferry Blues.

Come into the parlor

What you find in the *Official City Guide* of New Orleans is basic and historical, but not given to much detail. It has pride and a compressed set of facts, but you'd hardly guess that two sexes existed in the place, or that it was notorious because of it.

> *New Orleans in southeastern Louisiana, on the Mississippi River, 40 miles north of the Gulf of Mexico. The original settlement was founded by Sieur de Bienville and named for the Duke of Orleans. In 1762, against the wishes of French inhabitants, New Orleans was ceded to Spain. In 1803 it was given back to France and twenty days later ceded to the United States under the terms of the Louisiana Purchase. The city was twice subjected to military assault. In 1815 General Andrew Jackson successfully defended it against a British attack at the Battle of New Orleans—the final engagement of the War of 1812. In 1862 the city, a Confederate stronghold, was captured and occupied by Union forces. Its position has brought New Orleans prosperity and today it is the chief cotton market of the United States and one of the great ports of the world.*

There is a hint of a real New Orleans, the New Orleans of legend, of a past colorful and snapping its fingers, but that, too, is played down in the official text. The color and the careless laughter is missing, the vice is hinted at, the music put in quotes, the past done over to trap the tourist's dollar, giving him a hope that is sometimes gratified but usually diluted.

> *New Orleans prides itself as the "Most Interesting City in the United States" and the claim is justified. Famous for its Creole cuisine and fine restaurants, its* Vieux Carré *(Old French Quarter), its night clubs and "dixieland jazz." The city does have a great deal to offer. It's sophistication "honky-tonk" and Southern hospitality — all blended to make New Orleans a unique American city.*

There are of course *other* guidebooks, but some of them are long out of print, and often you will be told "they never existed." In 1902 *The Blue Book* appeared and for the next few years a new edition of it was issued each year. It was about six by five inches, ran to nearly 50 pages, and was sold for twenty-five cents in railroad stations, saloons, and on the steamboat landings. It contained pictures and text describing the sporting houses of New Orleans, the madames and the girls, the music and the sinful fun to be had there. There was also a section where the better joints advertised their attractions, decor, stars, and settings. Unlike ordinary guidebooks, it began with a firm notice:

THIS BOOK MUST NOT BE MAILED

> To know the right from the wrong, to be sure of yourself, go through this little book and read it carefully, and then when you visit Storyville you will know the best places to spend your money and time, as all the BEST houses are advertised. Read all the "ads."

4

Sporting House Row

The *landladies* were the madames of the houses and the women were the whores who worked in the sporting houses. *The Blue Book* was a serious publication, at least in its preface which even had a Latin motto, and it got right down to business as to why the book was needed and how to use it:

PREFACE
"Honi Soit Qui Mal y Pense."

This Directory and Guide of the Sporting District has been before the people on many occasions, and has proven its authority as to what is doing in the "Queer Zone."

WHY NEW ORLEANS SHOULD
HAVE THIS DIRECTORY

Because it is the only district of its kind in the States set aside for the fast women by law.

Because it puts the stranger on a proper and safe path as to where he may go and be free from "Holdups," and other games usually practiced upon the stranger.

It regulates the women so that they may live in one district to themselves instead of being scattered over the city and filling our thoroughfares with street walkers.

It also gives the names of women entertainers employed in the Dance Halls and Cabarets in the District.

The advertising section was neat and solid and the sell was soft without being chintzy—long before Madison Avenue had politely set down rules of the use of prose styles in attracting customers. Most of the famous madames, we suspect, wrote their own copy (those who could read and write). There were dim photographs of their Victorian and General Grant (or Robert E. Lee, it being the South) mansions and houses, whose exteriors presented facades as neat and ornate or balconied as

Private Party

any banker's residence back home—except for a red light of
ruby glass usually fed at the turn of the century by a gas jet.
The advertising had a period flavor suggesting bicycles, pug
dogs, Turkey red rugs, polished brass *and* flagellation:

MISS JOSIE ARLINGTON

225 Basin Streat   **Phone 1888**

Nowhere in this country will you find a
more complete and thorough sporting establishment than the Arlington.

Absolutely and unquestionably the most
decorative and costly fitted out sporting palace
ever placed before the American public.

The wonderful originality of everything
that goes to fit out a mansion makes it the
most attractive ever seen in this and the old
country.

Miss Arlington recently went to an expense
of nearly $5,000 in having her mansion reno-
vated and replenished.

Within the great walls of the Arlington
will be found the work of great artists from
Europe and America. Many articles from the
Louisiana Purchase Exposition will also be
seen.

7

Some of the houses boasted three languages spoken, as one of the places fondly advertised trilingual fornication:

MME. EMMA JOHNSON

Better known as the "Parisian Queen of America," needs little introduction in this country.

Emma's "House of All Nations," as it is commonly called, is one place of amusement you can't very well afford to miss while in the District.

Everything goes here. Pleasure is the watch-word.

Business has been on such an increase at the above place of late that Mme. Johnson had to occupy an "Annex." Emma never has less than twenty pretty women of all nations, who are clever entertainers.

Remember the name, Johnson's.

Aqui si hable Espanola

Ici on parle francais.

Phone connection   331-333 N. Basin

MISS RAY OWENS "STAR MANSION"
1517 Iberville Street   Phone 1793

By far the handsomest and most modern Sporting House in the Crescent City. The Turkish room in this mansion is the finest in the South, all the furnishings and decorations having been imported by Vantine of New York especially for Miss Owens.

Her ladies are: Mildred Anderson
Georgie Cummings   Sadie Lushter
Madeline St. Clair   Gladys Wallace
**   Pansy Montrose, Housekeeper**

8

Research has shown that about half of the girls, like modern film actresses, changed their names to glamorous-sounding versions of ladies.

But where was jazz in all this—and how did it fit in? Food, wine, and music heated the blood of tepid middle-aged spenders, and the music had to be new and exciting. On the streets of New Orleans in the late nineteenth century a new music was being born.

The street "spasm" bands ragged a tune by taking one note and putting in two or three in its place. Buddy Bolden, a popular barber and the first of the jazz greats, made a song of ragtime out of the street cries:

Any rags
Any rags
Any rags
Ain't you got anything *today?*

The Parlor

Everybody who could made music. The string bass and cymbals were knocked around like drums, the horns and the piccolo and tuba and alto horn voiced the polyphony. It sounded good, not out of pitch the way some said. Everything got mixed: work songs, "Drop That Sack"; spirituals, "When the Saints Go Marching In." Even the fake songs, "Jump Jim Crow," "Ole Zip Coon," and "Hamfoot." The circus and minstrel bands made a trombone slide. Scott Joplin was making "Maple Leaf Rag." Mills did "Georgia Camp Meetin'" and cakewalks like "Whistlin' Rufus."

If you had no horns you played harmonica, flageolot, homemade guitar, kazoo. Music was fun, even in the graveyards; Cypress Grove and St. Josephs and the Lafayette. The band behind the wagon, black plumes on the hearse, playing "Free as a Bird" or "Nearer My God to Thee," and then home to "He Rambled 'Round the Town 'til the Butcher Cut Him Down." Everybody clapped hands. At Spanish Fort and Milneburg on Lake Pontchartrain one could hear a classic stomp, "Milneburg Joys."

Times were hard for the freed slaves, and by 1900 *Freedom Now* was still a mockery. They were poor, uneducated, workbroken, often diseased, and all that was left was drink and their own music. Drink cost money, so you played your music to earn it if you could. Nobody called it an art form then, or a folk art, although they were already beginning to speak of it as "whorehouse music." But to the makers it was pleasure music.

From the picnic park of the New Basin Canal and wide-open

Bucktown Sundays, they went uptown to Washington Park, trailing horn or toting bass, up to Carrollton Avenue. Or they were hired to ride a wagon with a band and play to announce riverboats or fighters in the ring. The bands marched twelve to eighteen men. Four cornets, maybe, alto horn, E-flat cornet, E-flat clarinet. For dancing, smaller groups were enough, and noisy. The cornet on the legato runs and the arpeggios did the breaks, the trombone going into the slides. There could be a fiddle, drums, guitar and string-bass. The piano wasn't there much until 1900.

> Hard luck poppa standin' in the rain;
> If the world was corn he couldn't buy grain.
> Lord, Lord, got those Brown's Ferry Blues.
>
> Hard luck poppa standin' in the snow;
> His knees knock together but he's rarin' to go.
> Lord, Lord, got those Brown's Ferry Blues.

It was hardly a living unless a madame brought you into the parlor and let you cut loose; she paid you a little, let you take away the party leavings or pass the hat among the hincty gentlemen guests. The early times were hard days and blue nights for jazz struggling—hard to get dates and hard to own a good horn.

By 1890 jazz was there, and the New Orleans bands were growing. Small string bands—fiddle, guitar, mandolin, string-bass, and sometimes piano—were soon augmented to brass. They played popular stuff: waltzes, quadrilles, light classic, and, when they could handle it, operatic potpourri.

But from ragtime they slid into jazz, and the early jazz men said *to jazz* meant to fornicate, or, as they put it, (unaware the

Spasm Band

word is underworld jargon found in Chaucer and Shakespeare)
"jazzing meant *effing*." A "jazzbow" was a local Don Juan, and
as jazzing was available to all—one writer called sexual intercourse "the poor man's pocket polo"—it and the music were a
popular combination.

The great band of the early jazz was Buddy Bolden's. He
had been Kid Bolden and became King Bolden, and behind
him were others—the Excelsior Band, the Indian, Columbus
and the Diamond Stone bands. Born after the Civil War,
Buddy Bolden beat them all. He was a genius if folk art has a
genius, and he gave the music form, color, and showmanship.
Buddy was not modest, and he liked the girls and usually
traveled with three.

At the turn of the century there was plenty of room to create
jazz in the two hundred pleasure joints of Storyville, as the
legally accepted vice district, was called. There were cribs,
saloons, dancing schools, barrelhouses, creep dives, honky-tonks,
gambling set-ups. On Franklyn Street were big cabarets like the
101 Ranch, once the hangout of the roustabouts, pimps, and
big gamblers. As the games paid off, orchestras and entertainers were brought in. The best showed here. Joe Oliver,
Baquet, Bechet, Perez, Roy Palmer, Pop Foster, others who
were later some of the New Orleans "Rhythm Kings," "The
Halfway House," and "Original Dixieland Jazz Band." It was
long hours, small pay, but it was work and music.

Iberville Street had the 25 Club where the music boys hung
out with their horns and drank. Girls, chippie or singer or
entertainer in some Storyville house, the piano busy, somebody

Band Faces

giving it out, a cutting session starting the boys to jam. New tunes, gossip, good food. Pete Lata used the best; Zue Robinson, Henry Zino. Kid Ory ran a band there. So did Joe Oliver, and later when Oliver went to Chicago and there was need for a horn man, Louis Armstrong went there on Oliver's "come on up."

Jazz was slowly beginning to take form and create its music, but it wasn't respectable yet—the waltz was still king. Only the daring, the thrill hunters, the out-of-town sports, in "to change their luck" with a brown skin, heard the new music.

The first piano with a band was at Jack White's around 1900 in a tent on Iberville Street, a cabaret under canvas. The piano

15

player, Black Peter, couldn't play a tune, but he chorded, filled in rhythm. The real feisty places were the dance schools, taxi-dance halls, rub joints, where girls in skin-tight dresses danced with whomever stood them a drink. A bottle of beer was the cost and the dances were short, with time-outs for mauling the dolls and buying drinks. The honky-tonks were blue and raw. The 28 Club was the popular place; pimps, gamblers, and hired thugs gathered there. You could play faro, three-card monte, banco, and craps. It was a way-out place, blue-playing the music of the dives. On Pig Ankle Night the host handed out free pig's feet. Ham Kick Night saw a ham hung high on the ceiling and the gal who kicked highest and showed the

Dance Hall

most got the ham. When a dozen gals loaded on Red Eye were kicking, a Ham Kick was a wild dangerous thing.

> There's a big bull ring in the middle of the floor.
> A damned old jailor to close the door.
> Well, it's hard times in the Cryderville Jail.
> It's hard times, poor boy.

New Orleans was proud of its vice district: it was sanitary and protected the respectable town girls from indecent offers. It kept husband, father, and son from seducing the hired help. "Going down the line" on a Saturday night to the sporting houses was often a ritual for the southern male and his guests, more interesting than seeing the waterworks or Mr. Edison's electric lights on Canal Street. Usually wives, mothers, and virgins knew where the menfolk went. The whispered excuse behind many a respectable set of parlor drapes was: "Well yo' know menfolk—they just got to get rid of their high spirits and yo' can't ask a wife to act like a *hurr*."

So there was that part of town called Storyville, open for business, pleasure, vice, jazz. An ad for Tom Anderson's Cafe and Annex in *The Blue Book* stated: "Private dining rooms for the fair sex, all the latest musical selections nightly, rendered by a typical Southern darkie orchestra." Countess Willie Piazza bragged of her famous Mahogany Hall:

> The entire house is steamheated, and is the handsomest house of its kind. It's the only one where you get three shots for your money:
>
>> The shot upstairs,
>> The shot downstairs,
>> And the shot in the room . . .
>
> If there is anything new in the singing and dancing line that you would like to see while in Storyville, Piazza's is the place to visit. . . .

17

Jazz and women were not the only things. A handbill scattered widely over the town stirred sporting blood:

> Grand National rat-killing match for $100, to take place at Bill Swan's Saloon, corner Esplanade and Peters street, third district, Sunday afternoon at four o'clock precisely . . . a certain New York dog whose fighting weight is twenty-three pounds to kill twelve full-grown rats per minute for five consecutive minutes.
>
> **Admission, 50¢.   Reserved seats, $1.**

Music was often played at the sporting events, so jazz spread its wild notes. Madame Antonia P. Gonzales advertised her interest in fine music:

> The above party has always been a headliner among those who keep first-class Octoroons. She has the distinction of being the only Singer of Opera and Female Cornetist in the Tenderloin. She has had offer after offer to leave her present vocation and take to the stage. . . . Any person out for fun among a lot of pretty Creole damsels, here is the place to have it.

Did Antonia blow a hot jazz or play old French tunes? Or was she an early torchsinger? Details are missing, but from the notices music was a draw in the New Orleans sporting houses.

A great many books have been written as to how the Negro of New Orleans developed jazz, and the professors—the other ones, not the whorehouse piano players—are still not sure. The slaves came to town for fun before the Louisiana Purchase was in the history books. They came on their free time or stole away to the big field at Orleans and Rampart to horse and to laugh, to talk and find love. It was Indian country once, the old ceremonial grounds of the Oumas Indians. It became Congo Square. The white man calls it Beauregard or Circus.

Congo Square was a place to test a set of bones, the tom-toms—dancing and playing, shouting, *"Bamboula! Dansez! Bamboula! Badoum Badoum! Bamboula!"* Bamboula was the drum covered with cowhide, made of a length of bamboo. Before the brass, before the valve horns, they used a jawbone of the jackass, his teeth making a light rattle when hit in tempo. It could have started here as the bucks and girls horsed and rubbed each other

The Real Truth

in the dance and leaped high and wide. It had a little voodoo—
the French-speaking Negroes wore shoes, played in the little
orchestras, could say *"C'est le Congo! Fous-moi le camp!"*

There was work between music, mean work. And later came
the high-stacked packets, the gingerbread riverboats: stoke the
furnaces with pitch-pine, tote the bales, cut hair, wait on table,
run with mint juleps, and pour Bourbon. "Yes suh" and "yah
man." If they tipped, they were gentry and the quality. *"Yah
Yah Yah!"* the whites liked to hear it. When the band played
together it was on deck and the whites came to listen. River
music, black music. *Jazz!*

It had been going on for a long time and everybody thought
it would last forever—and no one could think of closing those
fine well-fitted houses on Basin Street. It was big business and
respectable folk collected the rent.

The Congo dances did end, and the boys got together on the
music. The Mississippi Delta was jumping with jazz, from the
humid city to the cypress forest, the palmetto thickets. It all
focused in the Nouvelle Orleans, the original town, the Vieux
Carré or the French Quarter. The Creoles of color were thickest
there, mixed bloods who sneered at the pure blacks but all with
a sense of music in their blood. The *menages*, the *mesamours*,
quadroon gals and French gentry had called for music and
laughter, and the black bands played at their parties and dances,
more freely than in solid white society; but they couldn't out-
draw the parlor houses and the sporting establishments.

Longstreet

Jamming

Perhaps advertising in *The Blue Book* made the difference.

> Minnie White, 221 North Basin, has surrounded her-
> self with a bevy of charming girls, each one a star,
> who are always willing to meet you half-way and
> make you feel that you are welcome.
>
> Alice Williams, 1545 Iberville, has a lot of jolly good
> girls as guests, who are the "goods" as one would
> term them. Don't overlook Alice.
>
> Countess Willie V. Piazza, 317 North Basin. If you
> have the blues, the Countess and her girls can cure
> them. She has, without doubt, the most handsome
> and intelligent octoroons in the United States.
>
> May V. Spencer, 315 North Basin, while very young,
> is very charming, and, above all things a favorite
> with the boys. . . . You should see her girls.
>
> Bertha Weinthal, 311 North Basin, while still young
> in years, has, nevertheless, proven herself a grand
> woman, and has also made "good" as a conductor of
> a first-class establishment.

How did this all begin?

New Orleans

Back Stage

Chapter 2

The Lay of the Land

The American Indians had their own story of how it all began, and before the French, the Spanish, the Americans, the sporting houses, the jazz men, the madames and the girls, even before the Indians, the river had to cut through the delta to pile up its silt—the world had to be made. The United States Bureau of American Ethnology gives the following Indian legend of creation:

> *Awonawilona—the Maker and Container of all, the All-father Father—solely had being. There was nothing else whatsoever throughout the great space, everywhere black darkness, everywhere void desolation.*
>
> *In the beginning the new-made Awonawilona conceived within himself and thought outward in space; mists of increase, steams potent of growth, were evolved and uplifted. With his substance of flesh drawn from the surface of his person, the Sun-father formed the seed-stuff of twin worlds, impregnating the great waters, and in the heat of his light the waters of the sea grew green, scums rose upon them, waxing wide and weighty until they became Awitelin Tsita, the four-fold containing Mother-earth and Apoyan Tachu, the all-covering Father-sky.*

Shanty Boat.

Anyone can see what had to come next, and how it was going to happen. The male and female elements had been created, the *yoni* and *lingan* of all life-giving, pleasuring, producing forces. Sex had entered the void, the firmament, the solid land, the green-scummed waters.

> From the lying together of these two upon the great world waters, vitalizing, terrestrial life was conceived; began all beings of earth, men and the creatures, in the four-fold womb of the world.
> Thereupon the Earth-mother repulsed the Sky-father, growing big and sinking deep into the embrace of the waters below, separating from the Sky-father in the embrace of the waters. A woman forebodes evil for her first-born ere born, even so did the Earth-mother forebode, long withholding from birth her myriad progeny and meantime seeking counsel with the Sky-father. "How," said they to one another, "shall our children, when brought forth, know one place from another?"

A good question. And one way to know and record is to give a place a name. Like Nouvelle Orleans.

No one knows very much about the Indians who lived in the muck of the great river delta on the gulf before the coming of the white man. They were not noble, brave, or much given to heroic action. They lived off fish and clams, in mud and hunger a great deal of the time. Trapping the water varmints and swamp game, cruel to their women, indifferent to their children, they were a miserable group of savages of no great virtue or valour. They were supposed to eat each other in hungry seasons. The fevers, the humid climate, and the wild river country did not make for a high culture.

Into this steamy wilderness of muddy waters, floating tree snags, bull 'gators, into the bayous came the French in 1777 as the Mississippi Company, because one of their early explorers had claimed it. The French province of Louisiana was named after a fat King Louis who walked on high red heels, rioted and orgied in a splendid court, and paved the way for a revolution to come down on future generations. This huge slice of French North America included all the land from the Ohio River down to the Gulf of Mexico, from the edge of the damned heretic English settlements in the east to the brutal slave-whip holdings of Spain in the west and south.

The French hadn't penetrated deeply into the muck of the delta. Since 1698 they had gone as far as what is now Mobile, the east bank of Biloxi Bay and the cliffs that were to be named Natchez. New Orleans was at first little more than a stockade and blockhouse, containing a motley population of about three hundred, of which over a hundred were soldiers, a few were scratching priests, and twenty-eight were women.

It is with these women that the sporting house history of the town begins. These were no ladies, no honest servant girls come out to find a husband. They were not pioneer women with axe and musket to stand by a man in a wilderness and cut down trees, raise up a brood of wagon-train bait or new Daniel Boones.

The women were frankly deportees, exiles shipped off, out of the prisons and whorehouses of Paris. Their companions were not solid citizens either, but wandering wild men of the rivers and forests, the *voyageurs* and *coureurs de bois*, pelt hunters and fur trappers drifting down from Canada. Between the rum, the exiled harlots, and the dull humid garrison duty in a far place, there was trouble, fighting, even murder.

Old Ruin.

Below New Orleans

The priests, seeing there were no souls to be saved here, suggested to the governor, Lamothe Cadillac (for whose family a luxury auto much favored by the madames was one day to be named) that all loose-living women be sent away. The governor issued the first public item on New Orleans women of easy and available virtue: "If I send away all the loose females, there will be no women left here at all, and this would not suit the views of the King or the inclinations of the people."

The women stayed on in flabby domesticity and greasy promiscuity. In tropical exile men seek drink, sex, and gambling. Since they were French, one is not sure in what order these things prevailed in Louisiana.

The town had been founded in Februaray 1718 on the site of a stinking Indian village, Tchoutchouma, set unideally in a cypress swamp and inhabited by animal life consisting of deadly snakes and snorting alligators. Convict labor was used, for not only women from prisons were being sent across the sea. Certainly if any city was founded by criminals, it was Nouvelle Orleans, as it was named to honor the French Regent, the Duke of Orleans. It was no pleasure city then. Governor Bienville recorded: "We are working at New Orleans with as much zeal as the shortage of workingmen will permit. I have myself conveyed over the spot to select the place where it will be best to locate the settlement. I remained ten days to hasten the works . . . I am grieved to see so few people engaged in a task which requires at least a hundred times the number. . . . All the ground of the site, except the borders which are drowned by floods, is very good, and everything will grow there."

They hoped for crops, rice in the mud; lobster, clams, and

crayfish were on hand. But tobacco and vegetables didn't do well in the drowned and flooded land. Cane brakes cut off sight and a man lost in them could hardly find his way out. Frogs were everywhere and fever banged in everyone's ears; for the deadly yellowjack came with the mosquitoes as the river flooded and lipped in over the land, drowning cattle and driving the whores and the convicts, the soldiers and the traders, into smoke-filled huts to battle chills and insects. It was a long way to the later sporting houses, and instead of jazz music the scraping and squeaking of a damp fiddle was the best that could be had. In winter, cold seeped into the flimsy huts; in summer the heat and humidity were unbearable. Mildew attacked supplies, leather melted and mold grew on everything. Water was the enemy; the soil was so saturated with it that even in death the poor whore and her germ collection could not be laid to rest properly. A traveler reports:

> *Coffins are therefore sunk three or four feet by having holes bored in them, and two black men stand on them till they fill with water and reach the bottom of the moist tomb. Some people are particular and dislike immersion after death; those who can afford it have a sort of brick oven built on the surface of the ground, at one end of which the coffin is introduced and the door hermetically closed, but the heat of the southern sun on this "whited sepulchre" must bake the body inside, so that there is but a choice of disagreeables after all.*

The first of the levees was built, but the river came in anyway, and a great deal of the time there was a foot of water in the town's muddy streets. There was still a shortage of true settlers. One historian explained how the government in Paris went to work to get citizens for the new land:

Field Hands

They went boldly to the task of ransacking the jails and hospitals. Disorderly soldiers, black sheep of distinguished families, paupers, prostitutes, political suspects, friendless strangers, unsophisticated peasants straying into Paris, all were kidnapped, herded, and shipped under guard to fill the emptiness of Louisiana. . . . To those who would emigrate voluntarily the Company offered free land, free provisions, free transportation to the colony and from the colony to the situation of their grants, wealth, and eternal prosperity to them and their heirs forever; for the soil of Louisiana was said to bear two crops a year without cultivation, and the amiable savages were said so to adore the white man that they would not allow these superior beings to labor, and would themselves, voluntarily and for mere love, assume all the burden of that sordid necessity. Endless variations were played upon the themes of gold and silver mines, pearl fisheries, a balmy climate that abolished disease and

Home.

old age, and a soil that had but to be tickled to give up almost as one wished, either the smiling harvest or the laughing gold.

And now the full tide of the boom began to reach Louisiana. The emigrants hurried out to fill seignorial rights, began to arrive in swarms and were dumped helplessly upon Dauphin Island.... Crowded, unsheltered and unfed, upon that barren sand heap, the wretched emigrants sickened, grew discontented, starved and died, yet there they had to wait until Bienville with his few boats and small force of efficient men could parcel them out about the country.... Faster than he could dispose of this mass of confusion, the infatuated enthusiasm in France continued to unload upon him and Louisiana.... To produce the human food required by the hungry octopus, the agents of the police scoured the kennels and alleys of Paris, and many a shipload of wretchedness was sent to the wilderness.

There was still a shortage of women, so the soldiers, convicts, and the Canadians (a lusty lot) raided Indian villages for women, even going as far as buying girls and women from the drink-hungry Indian men. The marriage of some Frenchmen to Indian squaws shocked the governor, although there were rumors, not recorded in formal history, that he was given to being comforted by a plump mulatto slave girl. (Still, perhaps one had to draw the color line in public.) He dispatched a hasty note to France, shrill in its cry for segregation, the first such message we have against integration in the South: 'Send me wives for my Canadians. They are running in the woods after Indian girls." (And catching them.)

In 1721, despite the royal edict against deporting riff-raff and sluts in force, eighty-eight girls were sent, mostly inmates of La Salpetriere, the house of correction in Paris, under the care of three nuns of the Gray Sisters, *and* a midwife, Madame Doville,

35

nicknamed *La Sans-Regret*. Governor Bienville wrote cheer-fully:

> *Nineteen of them have been married off. From those who came by Le Chameau and La Mutine, ten have died. So that fifty-nine girls are still to be provided for. This will be difficult, as these girls were not well selected.... Whatever the vigilance exercised upon them, they could not be restrained. Among the three Directresses responsible for their conduct, two have occasioned complaints. Sister Gertrude is ill-natured, she rules sourly and capriciously, and has been guilty of a prank which cost her the respect of the girls themselves. Sister Marie has none of the talents required for such responsibilities. Sister Saint-Louis has been retained, having a very good character.*

Sometimes the prostitutes are confused with another class of girl who was sent out to the colony. The tarts were called "correction girls" and the others *filles a la cassette*, "casket girls," chosen from middle-class families for housewifely duties and character. They were given a chest containing two coats, two shirts, undershirts, six headdresses, and other articles of cloth. The casket girls reached New Orleans in 1728 and continued to come until 1751. They were housed together and the men of the colony were permitted to see them by day; as night fell they were guarded by soldiers. Husbands were found for them. "This merchandise was soon disposed of so great was the want of the country."

All French families of Louisiana trace their descent from one of the *filles a la cassette* only. No Louisiana family has ever traced itself back to one of the bad girls, and one would think they had not reproduced. Actually they bred like minks, both the corrective girls and the casket emigrants. Some of the best

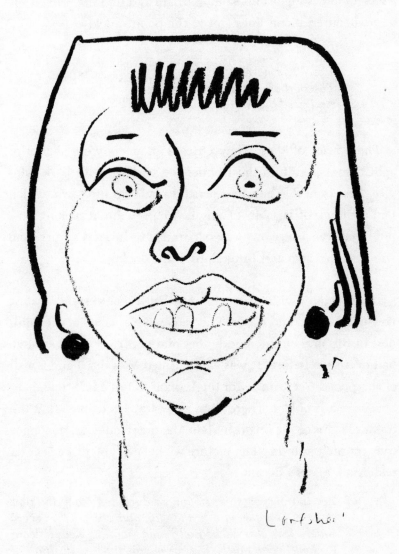

Lonfihen'

Reefer Smoker.

bayou society today is founded on a shipped-out harlot who mated most likely with a convict or a wild Canadian and in many cases created the proud Creole. The same situation existed in California in the days of the gold rush, and a wit, after observing a society in Pasadena and Santa Barbara and La Jolla pride itself on its honored blood lines, got to the point quickly:

> *The '49ers married*
> *The Barbary Coast whores*
> *And sired the Native Sons.*

The houses of these New Orleans pioneers were shacks of split cypress, built on the frontier log pattern, with bark shingles. Less than five hundred persons made up the town, which had a church of His Most Catholic Majesty and a reeking hospital that was a sure one-way trip to death. In 1723 a hurricane wrecked the town and three ships at the dock.

It was rebuilt without much hope that it would stand against new winds, fires, and floods .Travelers were amazed at the wildness of this city on the muddy toes of a vast river, such as none had ever seen before. It was a city armed by a ditch and a wall of sharpened tree trunks; for the Indians, if not a full-time menace, were a problem. There were also pirate raids now that the treasure ships of the Spanish Main, the great galleons, no longer came in such number. The picture we have of the place is not a real estate agent's dream.

> *For the purposes of draining, a ditch ran along the four*
> *sides of every square in the city, and every lot in every*
> *square was also ditched all round, causing New Orleans*
> *to look very much like a microscopic caricature of*
> *Venice.*

38

> *Mosquitoes buzzed and enormous frogs croaked inces-*
> *santly in concert with other indescribable sounds; tall*
> *reeds and grass of every variety grew in the street and*
> *in the yards, so as to interrupt all communication, and*
> *offered a safe retreat and places of concealment to ven-*
> *omous reptiles, wild beasts and malefactors, who, pro-*
> *tected by these impenetrable jungles, committed with*
> *impunity all sorts of evil deeds.*

The release from all this horror was still rum, women, and gambling. Those men who were able to get a casket girl had a private gold mine, the rest fought and orgied with the ragged sluts.

Unlike the Americans (one could no longer call the colonists English, even if the Revolution was still a good half century away), the French did not go much into the forest and explore the ridges and the Indian trails. They stuck to trading, planting, drinking, and whoring. The Americans were bold men in fringed buckskin, carrying Kentuck' rifles, drifting down the river in keel-boats and barges with corn and hogs, whiskey by the keg, pelts, and Indian finery, offering to trade and sell, and able to outdrink anyone in sight. Already the first river dens and dives were set up to entertain the Yankees, the bullboat men, the early sons of Mike Fink and the whole river crew that were never to stop coming down in their craft with their coonskin hats, wild songs, and shouts:

> *I'll never drink whiskey no more,*
> *Oh, I'll never drink whiskey no more,*
> *I'll lay me head in the barroom door,*
> *And I'll shout when I get happy, Lord, Lord.*

Even Abe Lincoln was to come a little later on with a boat-load of hogs to sell in New Orleans and to see his first slave market, see the various human beings sold for the marshes, the rice fields, or yellow girls for the beds of the gentry of the town and the plantations.

Scientists from France came from time to time to see what grew in this new world. They found strange plants, even a button tree whose nut served to hold up the pants and close the nightshirts of generations of Americans. One scientist found something that was like the Irish potato which he called "a white truffle, but much larger than the largest yam." It proved very potent when distilled into a native whiskey for the river dives, the first sporting houses.

Field Workers

Laundry

Respectable people hardly ever go out to a wild place to become colonists unless they are running for their lives, or their religion has been stepped on, or they are natural solitaries who want to go off and play at Robinson Crusoe. Greed will send men across the seas, but usually the wealth avoids them. The fur trader, the planter, were in the grip of the money lenders and the government grafters. Later the land speculator and the shark-eyed lawyer would take away, steal, most of what the first settlers had made out of the wilderness. As a wry backwoods philosopher once said:

41

It warn't the folk with the rifle and the hound dog who make themselves rich—it's the land thieves and the schemers and the banker and the lawyer. They see the biggety chance after the hard work and the dyin' has been done. They come in, grab it all from simple folk and settle down and run for public office. They set up the drinks in the hurrhouse and die easy in a feather bed and lay down in respectable graves.

There were respectable people in New Orleans, and folk dedicated to God and the Pope. Ursuline nuns had a nunnery there. The town was growing rich and the people who managed to make their pile imported good clothes and fancy furniture, carriages and blooded horses, and trained Negro house servants, picked for their looks, fine build, and ability to do what they were told with no sassy back talk. In 1827 Sister Hachard of the Ursuline nuns got a good glimpse of the town when it was beginning to take on character and get out of the log huts:

The streets are large and straight. The houses well built, with upright joists, the interstices filled with mortar, and the exterior whitewashed with lime. In the interior they are wainscoted. The roofs of the houses are covered with shingles which are cut in the shape of slates, and one must know this to believe it, for they all have the appearance and beauty of slate. The colonists are very proud of their capital. Suffice it to say, they sing here a song in the streets to the effect that this town is as fine a sight as Paris.

I do not, however, speak of the manners of the laity, but I am told that their habits are corrupt and scandalous. There, are, however, a great number of honest people, and one does not see any of those girls who were said to have been deported on compulsion. . . . The women here are extremely ignorant as to the means of securing their salvation, but they are very expert in the art of displaying their beauty. There is so much luxury in this town that there is no distinction among the classes so far

*as dress goes. The magnificence of display is equal to all.
Most of them reduce themselves and their family to a
hard lot of living at home on nothing but sagamité, and
flaunt abroad in robes of velvet and damask, ornamented
with the most costly ribbons. They paint and rouge to
hide the ravages of time, and wear on their faces as
embellishment small black patches.*

Most likely the innocent nun didn't know the patches were
often used to hide the sores of the old rale, as the disease of
Venus was called on the frontier. The French called it the Italian
Sickness, the Italians, the French Sickness, and both, when on
terms of peace, called it the English Sickness. The whores and
the sailors and soldiers helped make love a dangerous free-lance
game in the colony. Science had not yet discovered that there
were two major social diseases; so all were treated with mer-
cury, gunpowder-and-rum, and various other revolting mixtures.
The hardy natives first spoke of it with a phrase that was to
become native folklore: "No more bother than a bad cold."

The nuns were not poor. They were given land and eight
Negro slaves by the *Compagnie des Indies* which now ran the
colony. Six nuns went to the hospital as nurses, and they worked
hard bringing the one true religion to the yellow wenches, the
white tarts, the casket girls. Whores, being emotionally unstable
creatures, driven by circumstances beyond their control in those
days, were willing subjects for prayers, confessions, and masses.
The Negro girls were a little wary, and with downcast eyes listened and kissed the cross and said their "Hail Mary's," but
many, when they could, escaped to Congo Square for a few
hours of backsliding in the wild voodoo shouts and the hip-
swaying dances, then pairing-off with some laughing sweaty
buck in the tall grass.

New Orleans' reputation as a wide-open town was spreading, and outlaws fleeing Spanish and English laws came in growing number and looked about for prey. Murder was common, stealing a way of life. Every house had heavy locks, iron-bound doors, and few windows on the street. Property and life were always in danger.

Commander de Valdeterre of the French troops in Biloxi Bay painted a sad picture of the armed might of the French in Louisiana:

> *The troops are without discipline and subordination, without arms and ammunition, most of the time without clothing, and they are frequently obliged to seek their food among the Indian tribes. There are no forts for their protection; no places of refuge for them in case of attack. The guns and other implements of war are buried in sand and abandoned; the warehouses are unroofed; the merchandise, goods, and provisions are damaged or completely spoiled; the company as well as the colonists are plundered without mercy and restraint; revolts and desertions among the troops are authorized and sanctioned; incendiaries, who for the purpose of pillage, commit to flames whole camps, posts, settlements and warehouses remain unpunished; prisoners of war are forced to become sailors in the service of the company and by culpable negligence or connivance are allowed to run away with ships loaded with merchandise; other vessels are willfully stranded or wrecked and their cargoes are lost to their owners; forgers, robbers, and murderers are sure of immunity. In short, this is a country which to the shame of France be it said, is without religion, without justice, without discipline, without order, and without police.*

Chapter 3

On the Slave Block

What a terrible life I am led
A dog has it better
That's sheltered and fed
Night and day it's the same
My pain is their game—
Me wish to the Lord me was dead.

Somebody set that down to music in the middle of the eight-
eenth century, somebody who felt for the slaves enough to
know they were human, that they had feelings.

Whatever's to be done
Poor black must run—
Mungo here, Mungo there,
Mungo everywhere.
Above and below—
Sirah come, sirah go.
Do so and do so
Me wish to the Lord me was dead.

45

Picnic Fight

Except for modern Arab countries, brutally depraved—America was most likely the last nation to be built largely on slave labor. In the colonies the white slaves came as indentured servants, usually out of the gaols of Newgate and Kings Bench, often in chains, and their slavery was for a stated number of years. They farmed and crafted a great part of the early nation. Many of them stole a rifle or worked out their time, and went west to the Kentucky grounds and the Ohio country and beyond. But for the black man slavery was for life; few were ever set free, and even when one was, some crafty slave dealer and lawyer could often figure out a way of forfeiting freedom for a person who could not read legal documents or understand courtroom jargon.

Yet in time the slaves grew lighter and the white families here and there darker. For there was a slipping across the color line. The Couilles are also pioneers. The field hand's life was hard work, whip, discipline, and monotony. The daily routine on a plantation was a horn blown an hour before daylight. All workhands were required to rise and prepare their cooking for the day. The second horn was blown just at good dalyight, when it was the duty of the driver to visit every house and see that all had left for the fields. At dusk slaves returned to their quarters. Small children were cared for by elderly slave women. A former slave girl remembers the raising of children of all shades of color:

> I was Aunt Hannah's helper, and each morn' mama would drap me past Aunt Hannah's house. Guess they was 'fourteen chilun she had to look after. You ain't gonna believe dis, but it's de gospel truf. Aunt Hannah had a trough in her back yard—just like you put in a pig pen. Well, Aunt Hannah would just po' dat trough full of milk and drag dem chilun up to it. Chilun slop up dat milk just like pigs.

The slaves lived in fear of the auction block. They were sold for profit or punishment. Laborers on cotton plantations lived in terror of being "sold down the river" to the malaria-ridden rice swamps of Louisiana.

The owner of the following valuable slaves ran a newspaper announcement in 1835:

> ... being on the eve of departure for Europe, will cause the same to be offered for sale. ... Among the slaves are Dandridge, a mulatto, aged 26 years, a first-rate dining room servant, good painter and rough carpenter, and has but few equals for honesty and sobriety; Nancy, his wife, aged about 24 years, a confidential house servant, good seamstress, mantuamaker and tailoress, a good cook, washer and ironer, etc.; Mary Ann, her child, a creole, aged 7 years, speaks French and English, is smart, active and intelligent.

Most likely Mary Ann was fathered by her mother's master, now offering her for sale. Money was thicker than blood at a slave sale.

For the black man, brought across the sea in the hold of a stinking blackbirder, it was pure hell. The slaves from Africa were usually sold to the white buyers by other black people; the chiefs and witch doctors. They were often put naked on the block for sale, fingered and probed like hogs. In New Orleans, chained together, they lived in reeking barracks until sold, separated, and carried off. They were often flogged on their way to the rice fields or the tobacco patches, or they were put into clothes and made into house servants. The women were inspected like breeding mares, vent to nose, and treated like them if they had the looks and the fire.

Family Group

The slaves were kept ignorant; in fact up to the Civil War, in many sections of the country, it was a hanging offense to teach a slave to read and write. Some of the more handsome youths were kept like stallions for the human breeding pens; there were plantations that raised slaves like cattle or prize dogs for sale, and each buck had to impregnate his quota of girls. The resulting suckers (as the children were called) were fed and clothed, their skins oiled, and every season were moved from the breeding farms, usually toward New Orleans. They were trained as blacksmiths and carpenters, and the biggest and strongest as prizefighters and coachmen. The girls were ladies' maids, cooks, sewers of ballgowns. But mostly they worked the fields, carried the bales, lived in rags, and ate grits and mush and greens. They slept on pallets in cabins with earth floors. They died in the fever fields, drowned in the rivers, and, if sullen or sassy, were flogged to death or seared with hot irons, even castrated like gelding colts.

The life of the pretty slave girl could be easy for a few years, but when she thickened or was past her prime, she and her pale children often went to the slave trader's pen. That the nation that had produced the Marquis de Sade should have the normal number of hedonists, perverts, jaded and sated hunters of sensation was to be expected. And the details of the sins and outrages committed on slave bodies were more numerous than has ever been admitted. A native *Psychopathia Sexualis* would be the equal of an older civilization's texts.

About all that the white masters shared with the slaves, besides their bodies, was their religion. It cost nothing and the slaves were given a warped version of Christianity. In time they sang their songs of the Jews in Egypt, Them Golden Stairs or Slippers, and other themes they extracted from the Bible stories they heard. They made a sad fine music of it; they drummed to it and danced to it. Mostly they just clapped their hands and the music had the quality of being sad and yet rich, of being earnest and simple as they were; slaves, ignorant in exile, in a land for them as bad as Egypt.

> *The river of Jordan is mighty cold.*
> *It chills the body but not the soul.*
> *All my trials, Lord, soon be over.*

From the woodsy-pine men who came down the river and the wilderness folk who drifted down in flatboats the slaves heard the verses and the Elizabethan sound of *Barbara Allen* and other such ballads. From the hunters' songs and their own work songs and hollers and river songs and bale-lifting shouts, they began to assemble a music that was theirs and just theirs. But it had American roots. Only they were not yet Americans, not even French, not anything but living in New Orleans or along its delta and bayous, fetching for the whites in their damp and muggy city.

If they were house servants they knew the balls and the fetes and the drinking bouts and duels, "seegar" smoking and after-dinner brandy. And if they could be taught tunes they would play little French airs in polite orchestras, even light opera. If the slaves were craftsmen they shod horses, bowed and lifted their caps and saw the auction block where they had been sold to a bidder and might be sold again.

> *If religion was a thing that money could buy,*
> *The rich would live and the poor would die.*
> *All my trials, Lord, soon be over.*

Dixieland

A black flood was to stain North America; fifty years after the first cargo of Africans came to Jamestown the landowners imported more Negroes. Not until 1661 was slavery officially recognized as legal in the colony. The colonists realized the great potential of Negro labor. Negroes were being imported at the rate of 1,000 a year. In 1715, when the white population of the colony was 72,000, the Negroes totaled 23,000.

The growth of the Negro population caused the colonists to become worried about the mixing of the races. The first important legal distinctions between Negroes and whites were made in the 1660's. In Maryland, because white and Negro servants lived in the same quarters, the colonists found it necessary to pass the first law against miscegenation. In Virginia the child would have the same racial status as his mother; this protected the colonists from themselves by insuring that the children of planters and female slaves would join the minority race.

Fears of Negro uprisings, too, were intensified in 1687 by the discovery that slaves at Northern Neck, Virginia, were plotting to kill their masters. Severe slave codes were written into law. In 1707 the Virginia Slave Code declared that slaves were to be counted as "real estate," so that slave families could be separated. The Codes of 1748 and 1753 stated that no slave was allowed to leave the plantation without written permission. Slaves found wandering were to be returned. Slaves found guilty of murder or rape were to be hanged and their masters compensated by the colony. Robbery of a store or house by a slave was punished by sixty lashes; the culprit was placed in the pillory for half an hour: his ears were nailed to the posts, and finally his ears were cut off. For petty offenses slaves were whipped, maimed, or branded.

If you don't believe me, try it yourself;
Well, I tried it and I got left.

A prime black man could be worth $1,100 on the block in New Orleans, only $350 in Cuba—so the Negro increased his worth by a sea trip. Original music was bound to happen when the slaves got their drumming and singing mixed with Italian, Dutch, and English ballads and madrigals. The cotillions went down the hill to the slave cabins to become jigs, and when the first organ got into a church those notes weren't going to be lost.

The mountain and hunting men were loud in the river dives:

Blow your horn and call your dog
We'll go back to the woods
And catch a ground-hog.
Rang-tang fiddle-de-day.

The slaves added their personal lament:

Everybody strivin' to buy
Cheatin' each other
Me I cannot tell why
It's hard, hard times. . . .

The Negro slave had his public moments. The white entertainers would soon blacken up. In 1795, Gottlieb Graupner came from Hanover, Germany, discovered that he liked banjo music, and got into blackface in Boston's Federal Street Theater calling himself "The Gay Negro Boy." Another fake darkie in the 1800's was Thomas "Jim Crow" Rice:

Wheel about, turn about,
Do just so,
And every time I wheel about
I jump Jim Crow.

54

Banjo Boy

The slaves lived under the horror, yet even had their fun. They went out on Lake Pontchartain and laughed on Fat Tuesday, called Mardi Gras. It was a town for watermelon-pink colors, coffee and saffron-colored girls, and little drinking dives where they came to look at the colored man on a banjo strumming in memory of the plantation music. All along the gulf coast the little box banjos and tin whistles made music. Some place the bamboulas were beating out the beat, and Congo Square was the place. New Orleans was the pappy of it in Shantytown, among crap-shootin' sport, Creole yellow, big-footed mule driver, cotton hand, the colored boys in the boxing rings.

Slavery increased only when the white settlers failed to make things pay. The whites cost the French the sum of 150,000 livres a year to keep them in New France, and they were too lazy or sick to do much work. More and more slaves were needed. The Indians were worthless as slaves. They just sat and willed themselves to die in their chains, or they ran away or killed and were flogged to death without a sound of protest most of the time. You couldn't make a hoe-hand out of the Indian, or trust him as a house servant not to take the children's scalp or rape the mistress. It was the same everywhere in North America; attempts to enslave the Indians were unsuccessful. So they turned to Negroes. The importation of blacks was begun in 1712, and continued. The Company sold the slaves at prices from 660 to 676 livres, "on reasonable terms." A French official in 1724 estimated the black population at 3,300, and that of the whites at 1,700. Negroes captured by slave traders in Africa were mostly un-tamed savages from the jungles of the Congo. Stringent laws were enforced. In January 1724 came the *Code Noir*, Black

Shouter

Blues

Code, adapted from the laws of Santo Domingo, and also the basis of the Black Code adopted by Louisiana *after* the purchase of the territory by the United States. The most severe penalties were provided and inflicted in case of any act on the part of slaves which tended to endanger the absolute supremacy of the white race.

The Code began with a little extra bigotry thrown in. The first article of the Black Code ordered the expulsion of all Jews for no good reason at all. Other articles prohibited any form of worship but the Roman Catholic and instructed masters to impart religious instruction to their slaves. They provided for the confiscation of blacks placed under a person not a Catholic, or found at work on Sundays or holy days. The remaining articles dealt with the government and the Negroes. The Code, as window dressing, prohibited mingling of the races, concubinage with slaves, marriages of whites and blacks, free or slave, forbidden under penalty of fines and punishment. The manumission of slaves could be granted by masters over twenty-five, permission first obtained from the Superior Council.

The final article provided that "Manumitted"—freed—slaves are granted the same rights, privileges, and immunities which are enjoyed by free-born persons. It is our pleasure that their merit in having acquired their freedom shall produce in their favor, not only with regard to their persons, but also to their property, the same effects which our other subjects derive from the happy circumstance of their having been born free."

Naturally there was Indian trouble as the whites pushed back the natives. The wars were badly fought. Most of the French seemed to be women-hunters rather than fighters. One report speaks of the misconduct of the commander's favorites, Lesueur and the Jesuit, Father Beaudoin, "who to the great scandal of the Choctaws seduced their women." The randy monk of popular storytelling was often true to life. Nobody wanted to work, and seduction and drink and gambling were the prime doings. The governor could only tear at his wig and report:

> I neglect nothing to turn the attention of the inhabitants to agricultural pursuits, but in general they are worthless, lazy, dissolute, and most of them recoil from the labors necessary to improve the lands.
>
> The mortality of cattle is frightful, the drought is excessive, and the heat is suffocating. Such hot weather had never been known since the foundation of the colony, and it has now lasted four months without any change. From Christmas to the Saint John the waters were very high, so that many of the levees were broken. The one which is in front of the city gave way, and we were very near abandoning our houses and taking lodgings in boats. Then the drought came, and the river went down fifteen feet—a circumstance which had never been seen before. Hence the mediocrity of our crops.

Throughout the years vice was often the only paying business for those who lacked capital, land grants, or friends in France. New Orleans under the Marquis de Vaudreuil became a sort of criminal's playground. The whores, counterfeiters, innkeepers (with their ears cut off for crimes) all came down on the town from every part of the continent. It seemed as if there were no law on the delta that could touch the incoming mobs.

> Hangman, hangman, slack your rope,
> Slack it for a while.
> I think I see my mother coming
> Traveling many a mile,
> Lord, travelin' many a mile.

Soulsavers

I have brought the silver;
I have brought the gold.
I have brought you everything
To keep you from the gallows pole,
Lord, to keep you from the gallows pole.

In June 1751 the Intendant-Commissary told a sad story with its charges against the Marquis:

> He is too lazy, too negligent; his wife is too malicious, too passionate, and has too strong interests in all the settlements, and in the the town of New Orleans, not to prevail upon him to keep on fair, and even on servile, terms with the body of officers, and with others. . . . There is no discipline; the most indulgent toleration is granted to the soldiers, provided they drink their money at the licensed liquor shop where they are given drugs, which ruin their health; for several months there has never been less than a hundred of them at the hospital. . . . The soldiers are allowed to do what they please, provided they drink at the liquor shop designated for them; and they carry out of it wine and spirits, which they resell to the Negroes and to the Indians. . . . It is Monsieur Belleisle, the aid-major, who has the lease and adminis-tration of the liquor shop, and who gives for it a certain sum to the Major—others say to the Governor's lady. What is positive is that Monsieur de Vaudreuil has drawn upon the treasury for ten thousand livres of his salary as Governor, which he has given to Monsieur Belleisle, and it is with these funds that the supplies of the liquor shop have been bought. . . . Moreover, Madame de Vaudreuil is capable of carrying on a still baser sort of trade. She deals here with everybody, and she forces merchants and other individuals to take charge of her merchandise and to sell it at the price which she fixes. She keeps in her house every sort of drugs, which are sold by her steward, and in his absence she does not scruple herself to descend to the occupation of measure-ment and to betake herself to the ell. The husband is not ignorant of this. He draws from it a handsome revenue, which is his sole wish and aim.

Another report declares:

> *The province has been handicapped by drunkenness, brawls and duels by which half the population was destroyed, the morals of the military, and a shameful system of plunder authorized by the Governor. Officer-kept mistresses were received at the Governor's mansion above the wives of colonists. Officers went about the streets wearing nightcap and nightshirt.*
>
> *Thieves and prostitutes formed a large disturbing group of Louisiana's inhabitants. New Orleans became the resort of vicious criminals devoted to stealing and drinking in pot houses and taverns, and dens along the river and the swamps. During the next century one third of the city was given over to vice and crime. By 1750 a great deal of the paper money in the province was found to be counterfeit.*

This brought in a reform movement; thirty articles of control were published to take care of public vice, the whores, the criminal hangouts in the unlicensed drinking joints. Innkeepers were warned against giving aid to runaway slaves or teaching them the art of stealing. Negro and mulatto women were not to be forced into brothels or the lives of prostitutes. That's what the law said. It bore down on the Negroes:

> *All free Negroes and Negresses, living either in the purlieus of this town or in its vicinity, who may become guilty of harboring slaves, in order to seduce them and excite them to plunder their masters and lead a scandalous life, shall lose their freedom and become the slaves of the King. . . . Any Frenchman who shall be so infamous as to become guilty of the offenses described in the preceding article shall be whipped by the public executioner and, without mercy, sentenced to end his life on the King's gallows. . . .*
>
> *No drunk-making beverages to be distributed or drunk in, or carried away from, any private house.*

Mom and Dad

Six taverns are to be established in New Orleans under commission issued by the Governor.

Tavern keepers not to sell liquor to soldiers, Negroes, or Indians.

Taverns to be closed Sundays and holidays during divine worship, and at nine o'clock in the evening.

Two liquor shops established for the exclusive use of soldiers. One French, the other Swiss. To be operated by the officers in command of the respective companies.

All persons who have left their fields to settle in New Orleans must return home within eight days, or be driven from the city as people of an infamous character.

It all came to very little. The few places that were closed soon paid off to the right people and reopened, and with the ink hardly dry on the new laws, rum dens, gambling houses, and brothels, were as busy as ever.

Times were changing. In Europe their Catholic Majesties were busy killing each other's subjects. Spain was looking to the New World, trying to seize what was left on the North American continent. The French had fought the British, and the Spanish were harassing the French. Every place there were soldiers and ships, fleets and bronze cannon. There was talk in New Orleans of forming a union with the English colonies and tossing off the rule of Europeans. But the Americans were not yet ready.

On one of those humid days, August 18, 1769, Don Alexander O'Reilly, an Irish general in the service of Spain, landed at New Orleans with twenty-four warships, three thousand soldiers, and fifty pieces of artillery. It was a full hand in poker. The Superior Council held ceremonies in the Place d'Armes. General O'Reilly took over Louisiana in the name of the King of Spain.

The slaves, the thieves and the prostitutes knew that for them nothing would change but the language.

> *I've brought you no silver:*
> *I've brought you no gold;*
> *I've come for to see you hangin'*
> *Hangin' from the gallows pole,*
> *Lord, hangin' from the gallows pole.*

BOOK TWO

THE CITY

Sporting House

Chapter 4

The Yanks Are Coming

> *All de doctors you can try*
> *All de medicine you can try*
> *You gotta lay down*
> *Some day*
> *And die . . .*

The Spanish began by condemning to death by hanging then by shooting twelve local revolutionists, almost ritual in any Latin country even today. General O'Reilly went to work putting some order in the city, taking a census among the people; and all the time the shouters in the marketplace continued singing their wares.

> *Oysters. She crab!*
> *Raw shrimp*
> *Raw, raw*
> *Raw!*

The figures showed a population of 3,190 persons in New Orleans. Among them, there were 1,225 Negro slaves and 60 Indians. Under the Spanish law Indians could not be held as slaves. Of free citizens, 31 were Negroes and 68 were of mixed blood. The town contained 468 houses on four streets next to the Mississippi. The province, including New Orleans, held 13,538; half of these were slaves. During the war with England hundreds of French colonists fled to New Orleans. Immigration of Acadians expelled from Nova Scotia by the English who treated the province as another India brought honest folk to New Orleans. Twenty came in 1764, followed by 650 in 1765. Settlements were established at Attakapas and Opelousas. By 1787 there were 1,587 Acadians in Louisiana.

O'Reilly organized as a governing body the Very Illustrious Cabildo, six perpetual regidores (aldermen), two alcaldes, (judges) and an attorney-general. The governor presided in person over these officials. By special proclamation O'Reilly kept the Black Code as a law of the land. Maintaining law and order in the settlements was the Santa Hermandad, or Holy Brotherhood, acting as judge and executioner. The law declared:

> *The principal object of the institution of the tribunal of the Santa Hermandad is to repress disorders and to prevent the robberies and assassinations committed in the unfrequented places by vagabonds and delinquents, who conceal themselves in the woods from which they sally to attack travelers and the neighboring inhabitants. The Alcalde Mayor Provincial shall assemble a sufficient number of members of the Santa Hermandad to clear his jurisdiction of the perpetrators of such evil deeds, by pursuing them with spirit, seizing, or putting them to death.*

Listed as crimes were:

> *He who shall revile our Savior, or His mother the Holy Virgin Mary, shall have his tongue cut out, and his property shall be confiscated, applicable one-half to the public treasury and the other half to the informer. Flogging, confiscation of property for anyone vilifying the King or any member of the royal family. A commoner's use of scurrilous language to the detriment of another citizen is subject to a fine of 1,200 maravedis. For a nobleman who commits a similar offense the fine is 2,000 maravedis. A married woman caught in adultey and her partner in sin are delivered up to the husband to be dealt with as he pleases. The law provides he cannot put one to death without the same punishment on the other.*

Taxes went up. There was a tax of forty dollars on each tavern, billiard table, coffee house; twenty dollars on each boarding house, one dollar on every barrel of brandy. There was a tax for the maintenance of the levee; six dollars on a boat of two hundred tons, three dollars on craft in the port. Brothels are not mentioned, but the police levied an unofficial graft to permit them to stay open.

Louisiana continued to be an international football. In October 1800, Spain gave the colony back to France, but the French were so busy that they didn't get there till 1803. During this period the town ran wide open, the criminals took over and entrenched themselves; the whores, gamblers, robbers, and pirates laughed at the civil guard and the *serenos'* efforts to keep law and order.

The most notorious dive in New Orleans was the Mal Maison Coquet on Royal Street, which was not only a house of prosti-

Street Holler

tution, dram shop, and gambling hell, but also a grocery store. Cabarets were popular, as were coffee houses where anything in the sexual field, murder, drugging, erotic shows of naked women copulating with humans and animals, and plain debauched drinking went on—all, as their public posters stated proudly, "by permission of the Honorable Civil Governor of the City."

The French arrived in March of 1803, but news came in July that Napoleon, in need of cash and fighting to stay top dog in Europe, had sold all of Louisiana and all his claims to the vast heartland of the continent to the new nation, the United States. Mr. Jefferson had made a keen bargain in land. But no one was too sure about New Orleans. Troops patroled the city night and day to keep down riots and looting. New laws came in, but the Black Code stayed. These fresh regulations tried to keep down the crime rate, control the whorehouses, punish criminals. They merely added a few more to the many unenforceable laws.

The market criers went about their business:

> *Vegetables, Guinea squash,*
> *To-mat-tuhs, Sibby beans!*
> *Hardhead cabbages,*
> *York cabbages!*

And in the dives there was an early version of:

> *I ain't goin' to do it no more,*
> *Oh I ain't goin' to do it no more.*
> *If I ain't been drinkin' so much whiskey,*
> *Wouldn't be layin' on this 'ere hard floor . . .*

The new Council's regulations, 108 articles, forbade cursing and driving carts on Sunday. No slaves, soldiers, or sailors were to be out in the city after eight o'clock at night in winter or nine o'clock in summer, without a written pass from master or officer. A cannon fired in the Place d'Armes was a signal for slaves to go home and soldiers and sailors to go to their barracks and ships. The signal was given until 1862, when it was abolished by the Union Army in New Orleans after the capture of the city by Farragut.

The New Orleans America acquired was a city of 4,000 houses and 10,000 inhabitants. Of these 5,000 were whites, 2,000 free Negroes, and the remainder slaves. The town was 600 yards wide and extended along the river. The stockade enclosed the town with forts at the corners. Canal Street was only a moat and a military gate on the Tchoupitoulas Road. The Cabildo, Arsenal and French Market remain almost as they were, facing the Place d'Armes, a grass lot. Wooden gallows stood where the statue of General Jackson is now. On Chartres Street stood the pillories that imprisoned the head and hands, or held the fingers of both hands with the joints bent. Anyone sentenced to the pillory sat on a platform, on his neck a placard: "My name is Frank Beris. I am a thief. I stole from Sam Hay. Sentenced to 5 days' exposure at the pillory." Rotten fruit and other trash was hurled at the occupant. The pillory was still in use as a punishment for Negroes as late as 1847.

The rest is history of an exotic, erotic kind. With the Americans the sporting house began to take on familiar important features. As in most American cities, the red-light district was admitted as being there, but nice people didn't talk about it. Under American order and efficiency the political and economic power of whorehouses lasted until the end of Storyville. The city government and the police soon saw the share-the-wealth plan inherent in prostitution and gambling. Each house, each gambling setup, over the years was scientifically assessed a certain sum, to be used in crooked elections and in moving the boodle so that every high official who would take was given. In return the sporting houses and dives were policed and protected. Outraged or robbed patrons were soothed, conned, or run out of town. Runaway whores were turned over to the police, sometimes effectively beaten up for the madames. In case of a reform administration or ticket, a few raids were carried out. Or if the opposition was weak, warning would come to the madames, the gamblers, and the saloon keepers that the raid was planned—get the girls and the untaxed booze and the crap tables and wheels out of sight.

> *I can't keep open*
> *I'm gonna close my shark*
> *The chief of police*
> *Done torn my playhouse down*
> *No use in grievin'*
> *I'm gonna leave this town . . .*

Such was the song of an unprotected place, an outlaw sporting house that tried to buck the official, paid-up places, and didn't have a fix in with the police or the city fathers.

> *Check all yo' razors*
> *An' yo guns*
> *We's gonna be wrasslin'*
> *When the wagon comes.*

Jitterbug

If there was one change that the Americans brought which bit a little deeper than most, it was their sense of sin while sinning. The French and the Spanish could run to confess and be forgiven after some vows to try to do better. But the Americans were held in some dark strain by the message of Jonathan Edwards, who had preached to the groans and tears of his listeners, of *Sinners In The Hands of An Angry God*. He laid it on like whiplashes, and Americans were touched; they suffered as they sinned and fornicated. He promised all a fearful end and described the other world waiting for them with the glee of a pornographer detailing his little games. There is something strangely sexual in Edwards' fury and preachings:

> *The God that holds you over the pit of hell, much as one holds a spider, or some loathsome insect over the fire, abhors you, and is dreadfully provoked; his wrath towards you burns like fire; he looks upon you as worthy of nothing else, but to be cast into the fire....*
>
> *O sinner! consider the fearful danger you are in: it is a great furnace of wrath, a wide and bottomless pit, full of the fire of wrath, that you are held over in the hand of that God, whose wrath is provoked and incensed as much against you as against many of the damned in hell: you hang by a slender thread, with the flames of divine wrath flashing about it, and ready every moment to singe it, and burn it asunder; and you have no interest in any Mediator, and nothing to lay hold to save yourself, nothing to keep off the flames of wrath, nothing of your own, nothing that you ever have done, nothing that you can do, to induce God to spare you one moment.*

It was a fearful thing to know one was so doomed and yet could not stop sinning, for the desire for fornication was often stronger than the will to be saved. The whore-user, adulterer, once having fallen, felt hopeless and sinned even more, knowing that he was lost, damned; in his ears the sound of that message scored his doom.

> *That awful spectacle, that they may see what the wrath and fierceness of the Almighty is; and when they have seen it, they will fall down and adore that great power and majesty. Isa. 66:23,24: "And it shall come to pass that from one moon to another, and from one Sabbath to another, shall all flesh come to worship before me, saith the Lord. And they shall go forth and look upon the carcasses of the men that have transgressed against me; for their worm shall not die, neither shall their fire be quenched, and they shall be abhorring unto all flesh."*

Doomed or uncaring, sinful or lusty, Americans were pouring west, away from the Eastern seaboard, two million of them crossing the mountains going west, filling in the empty land; many of them moving down river with canoes, skiffs called Mackinaws, keelboats, flatboats, broadhorns, arks, pirogues, scows; sliding onto sandbars, dying on snags and sawyers, stuck in mudbanks, pursued by river pirates. Bragging and drinking, steering south and singing:

> *I'm looking for the bully*
> *The bully of the town;*
> *I'm looking for the bully,*
> *But the bully can't be found:*
> *I'm looking for the bully of the town.*
>
> *And when I walk this levee round,*
> *I'm looking for the bully of the town.*

The goal was New Orleans, where the boats were broken up and sold as lumber, and when the pigs and whiskey and hides from a thousand boats a year were paid for, the wild crew went on the town to the whores and the gamblers, to the grog shops,

Lampstool   Dance Hall

barrel joints, and dance halls. Dance-hall smoke and rum and
naked women got a lot of the hard work coming down river.
Those who survived knives, guns, and drugged drinks and
didn't get the old rale went slowly home up-river in the new
steam packets or walked a "fur bit" if they were broke.

> *It's a long John*
> *He's long gone*
> *Like a turkey through the corn*
> *Through the long corn.*

With the steamboats coming it was easier to ride both ways,
and soon the tall stacked packets and sidewheelers were
coming around the bend, bring life to hundreds of dismal
settlements, every boy dreaming of piloting one down to New

Orleans, and even the girls whispering of the lure and color and all that sinning. A few even ended up in the sporting houses. When Eli Whitney came along with the cotton gin, so that the seeds no longer had to be picked out from the cotton bolls by hand, there was cash in the linen jeans and the white planter's suits. A good frisky place to spend it was New Orleans.

There was style there, and good food and fine bars of solid teak and mahogany. And best of all there were painted, scented, skilled women. The trek west was made by men of vitality and manliness; they had sexual drive to spare and the sporting houses were the goal of every full-blooded American boy in his secret troubled dreams. Even if he was church raised, or a minister's son, or had New England guilt, in his desires (repressed or not) he dreamed most of the honey-colored women's bodies available on the delta. A whole folk culture of sexual myths grew up about the place, of its sleek gamblers with cards up their sleeves, of whores of amazing abilities with "French" tricks and outrageous performances of all kinds of acts and their themes and variations. This, as much as the lure of gold, of making a fortune, drove boys to run away.

The legends grew of the dance-hall girl with a heart of gold, the harlot who supported a sick mother, who went to church on Christmas Eve, the madame whose folks in Pittsburgh thought she was a singer in a Protestant choir. The English duchess working in a whorehouse, the society girl who was sex mad and driven to the foulest cribs and the more bestial the customers the better—all of this became folk tradition. And there was *just* enough truth in it (not much but a touch) to make it part of the dogma of the sporting house trade.

Club Dance

Sociological study has shown that poverty, laziness, neurotic flaws, and often just the wish to please some man was what made whores in New Orleans, as elsewhere. Few were driven by flaming sexual needs, not many got any ecstatic reaction or pleasure for all their moaning and tossing and crying out ("Oh give it to me, give it *all* to me!"). It was great bedroom drama, but hardly an honest act of love. Orgasm-racked tarts could hardly keep in business. Their nervous systems would have shattered, to say nothing of the physical conditions of girls and women who in the low-river cribs took on forty to fifty customers a night.

Even in the plush houses a lady was expected to turn four or five tricks a night. A customer could buy a girl's time for the entire night, but that was a sign of sexual bragging. Usually the backwoods Don Juan on a spree liked to sample a few tasty items in a night, rather than confine himself to one dish. The town trade—the planter, merchant, city or government official—usually had a favorite house, a friendly madame, and a girl that was just his style and knew his needs. And if he was elderly or jaded, he was keenly interested in the byplay that brought him to climax, biological nirvana.

Negro and white whores, even if they worked for the same madame, were segregated in two separate houses usually next door to each other or across an alley.

> *Go 'way, go 'way, darlin' Corey.*
> *Quit hangin' round my bed.*
> *Pretty women run me distracted,*
> *Corn likker's killin' me dead.*

Inside Bourbon St

The word "Negro" was hardly a fair term, for there were whole rainbow hues of colors by which the girls were graded. Most of them were slaves, bought young and trained, or imported from up-river, or found in some backwater cathouse serving the bumpkins and rural studs. Most of the coffee-colored golden tans, beginner browns, high "yellas," claimed to be Creole spawned.

Explanation of the term Creole is needed here. The French oddly enough did not originate the term. It seems to be Spanish in origin. At first it referred to any native of Louisiana. In time it was used only for the descendants of those Spanish and French who had first settled the place. Whites and Negroes of the original settlers were both called Creole—even the animal life was called Creole hoss, Creole hog, Creole bull, and, of course, Creole nigger. In time the whites claimed to be the only true Creoles. However Negroes think of octoroons as Creoles, and as Mark Twain once put it: "A lot of the fancy quality down there that's so bigoted and busy with the Klan riders and keeping down the nigrah have a lot of colored blood bred in from the Creole days."

> *I ain't no high yaller, I'm a beginner brown*
> *Ain't gonna marry, ain't gonna settle down.*
> *Gonna drink good moonshine*
> *And run them browns down*
> *That long lonesome road, Lord,*
> *You know it's gotta end.*

The French and Spanish didn't care much for American push and direct action or Indian camp manners. Called *Americains*, they pleasured the girls, got drunk, wrecked the joints; when they tried to speak to the Creole girls of the respectable part of town, the kids would run after them howling:

> *'Méricain coquin,*
> *'Billé en nanquin,*
> *Voleur di pain*
> *Chez Miché d'Aquin!*

When the boats were swarming along the levees in season, the town was unsafe for proper citizens at night. And the cry rang out warnings to bad children: *"Toi, tu n'es qu'un mauvais Kaintock!"*

Flatboats, cargo-barges, and other vessels sold for lumber inspired some businessmen with the idea of moving the women and the drinking out to the boats. Soon a floating city of vice greeted the traveler before he could set foot on dry land. In narrow cabins with hastily built walls, on husk pallets, even on deck under wagon canvas, the prostitutes did their business, while Negro music came from gourd fiddles and battered horns.

> *Oh, come and buy now,*
> *I'm here today,*
> *Tomorrow I'll be gone.*

As the white man, visitor or citizen, played and larked, the Negro lived in another world—his half-white daughter carried off to the sporting houses, his wife debauched if she attracted the overseers, his sons made into beasts or prizefighters, he himself walking humble and barely above an animal level. A visitor, Frances Ann Kemble, has left us a clear picture of what the Negro suffered. Uncle Tom and Simon Legree were too black and white, too melodramatic. The truth was deadly gray:

> *These cabins consist of one room, about twelve feet by*
> *fifteen, with a couple of closets smaller and closer than*
> *the staterooms of a ship, divided off from the main room*
> *and each other by rough wooden partitions, in which*
> *the inhabitants sleep. Almost all of them have a rude*
> *bedstead, with the gray moss of the forests for mattress*
> *and filthy, pestilential-looking blankets for covering. Two*
> *families (sometimes eight and ten in number) reside in*
> *one of these huts, which are mere wooden frames pinned,*
> *as it were, to the earth by a brick chimney outside,*
> *whose enormous aperture within pours down a flood of*
> *air, but little counteracted by the miserable spark of*
> *fire, which hardly sends an attenuated thread of lingering*

Dead Mans Watch

smoke up its huge throat. A wide ditch runs immediately at the back of these dwellings. Attached to each hovel is a small scrap of ground for a garden, which, however, is for the most part untended and uncultivated.

Such of these dwellings as I visited today were filthy and wretched in the extreme, and exhibited that most deplorable consequence of ignorance and an abject condition, the inability of the inhabitants to secure and improve even such pitiful comfort as might yet be achieved by them. Instead of the order, neatness, and ingenuity which might convert even these miserable hovels into tolerable residences, there was the careless, reckless, filthy indolence which even the brutes do not exhibit in their lairs and nests, and which seemed incapable of applying to the uses of existence the few miserable means of comfort within their reach. Firewood and shavings lay littered about the floors, while the half-naked children were cowering around two or three smouldering cinders. The moss with which the chinks and crannies of their ill-protecting dwelling might have been stuffed was trailed in dirt and dust about the ground, while the back door of the huts, opening upon a most unsightly ditch, was left wide open for the fowls and ducks, which they are allowed to raise, to travel in and out, increasing the filth of the cabin by what they brought and left in every direction.

In the midst of the floor, or squatting round the cold hearth, would be four or five children from four to ten years old, the latter all with babies in their arms, the care of the infants being taken from the mothers (who are driven afield as soon as they recover from child labor), and devolved upon these poor little nurses, as they are called, whose business it is to watch the infant, and carry it to its mother whenever it may require nourishment. To these hardly human little beings I addressed my remonstrances about the filth, cold, and unnecessary wretchedness of their room, bidding the older boys and girls kindle up the fire, sweep the floor, and expel the poultry. For a long time my very words seemed unintelligible to them, till, when I began to sweep and make up the fire, etc., they first fell to laughing, and then imitating me. The *incrustation of dirt on their hands, feet and faces were my next object of attack, and the stupid Negro practice (a short time since nearly universal in enlightened Europe) of keeping the babies with their feet bare, and their heads, well-capped by nature with their woolly hair, wrapped in half a dozen hot, filthy coverings.*

It is no cause for wonder that the Negro turned to laziness, sluffing off his slave-made work, lying, stealing, giving the false *yak yak* laugh, comically shuffling along to keep the tempers of the white folk down, playing at being bone-head dumb.

No wonder his music is sad and blue, and that when he can, he will break out and become mean, even if they skin him with a black snake whip. Those who revolted suffered most. Those who grew wise to the white man's ways learned to bamboozle him and develop slyness. Women twisted their bodies and used them to better themselves. They drummed and danced sensually when they could. If there was whiskey, they drank it and filled up with water what they had taken. They abandoned themselves at times to lechery; at least it was available under certain conditions.

The young pretty boys, forced to pander to the whims of homosexual whites, developed mincing ways. The half-white mother told her near-white daughter to latch on to the white "massa" and make him a slave to her body; to ask for earrings and doodads, to hold back a bit and then enflame. It was deadly serious warfare, and the Negro fought it. He slowly saw himself diluted; red hair, blue eyes, different features began to appear in the slave quarters.

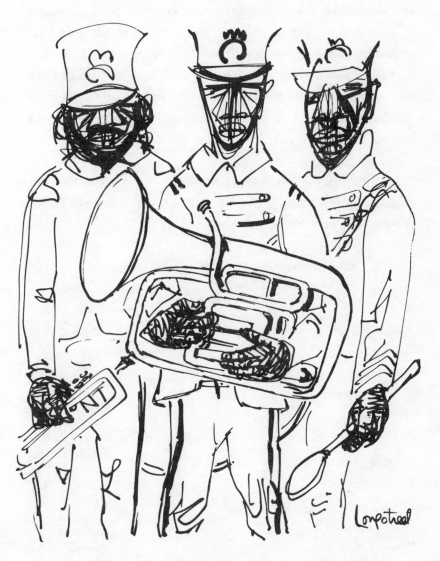

Circus Jazz

The Negro fought on, with drum and flute, with song and laughter. He stole, lied, went to his whitewashed shack of a church, wondering if God was black, or white. He didn't know or care that his music was one day to have value. It served him and it was his. It was about the only thing he owned. He was no saint and he was no monster; he loved his children and his woman as much as the master did his own household. He was no hero; he slid away from trouble and he didn't take blame that was rightly his. He didn't see how to face up to the whip and hound dog and overseer and his own ignorance. He could express himself only in fornication, dancing, and music.

A later jazz man, Jelly Roll Morton, was to say: "You just don't make the blues out of air but out of the corner of your head where everything has been put away."

> *Went across the river, lay down to sleep.*
> *Woke up with shackles on my feet.*
> *Twenty links of chain 'round my leg,*
> *On each link a letter of my name.*

Mardi Gras

Sailors Return

Chapter 5

Gone Are the Days

In the unpublished memoirs of a Storyville madame, calling herself Nell Kimball, there is reference to the wild rivermen and the district in New Orleans called The Swamp:

> *When I opened my house on Basin street in the early '80s you could still find people who said they remembered those wild rivermen when the flatboats were used as cribs for the hookshops and the hookers lived, slept, ate and boozed on the waterfront by that section of town where the flatboats looked on Tchoupitoulas Street. The Swamp began on Girod Street, some blocks from the river by the Protestant Cemetery at Cypress and South Liberty Streets. The Swamp was the favorite of the flatboat men, that and Gallatin Street, the toughest area ever in New Orleans.*
>
> *Old timers talking to me would have tears on their faces when they got to the charm of The Swamp. Ten to twelve people a week were done in there, and nobody gave a damn—or called the cops. The city didn't bother to make*

anything of it. The cops never came into The Swamp; it was a kind of unwritten law, if the vice didn't leak out into the hinchy, respectable part of the town. Girod Street, it didn't have no more law than any western town before the marshalls came in, and it was fighting with your teeth, handy-andy [blackjack], hogleg [pistol] or chiv [knife], your only friends in the Swamp.

The Swamp was a baker's dozen of blocks but real solid with whore houses, hot sheet hotels (rented by the hour), gambling joints, and dance halls where the girls carried chivs in their garters and their tits flopped out of their dresses and the Johns [customers] got a dry rub standing up. The places stank from manure, privies and the black mud street. The shacks were just old river barges broken up and used as lumber with the cypress planks raw-sawed.

A red lantern or even a curtain was the decoration, a board was a bar. An old hustler that worked all The Swamp in those days, peddling it, told me the price for a woman; a snort of corn whiskey and a kip [bed] for the night was one or two picayune [six cents was the value of a picayune]. Some men were given mickeys, rolled, sandbagged, and even killed and dropped into the river.

Gambling was always trouble for the whore. It kept men away from a girl's trying to make a score [plying her trade]. Crap shooting was popular, but for those who could add there was this faro and the wheel and the ivory ball. All the games were crooked, the dice capped for the chumps. A winner was pushed back with saying he had hidden cards, or he was followed out into the street and given a good headache with a stocking full of sand. The worst places were the House of Rest and the Weary Boatman. Not even a hooker was safe there. Many a hard working whore was stripped down and tossed drunk and without a stitch on into the alley.

We shall quote from Nell Kimball's memoirs from time to time, for her picture of the times and the sporting houses is the closest to the scene by a professional.

House Girls

She defines the name hooker for a prostitute in this way:

> The moniker hooker for a whore came about in the Civil
> War where everybody was far from home and looking for
> a bit of it. General Joe Hooker, a handsome figure of a
> man, was a real quif-hunter and he spent a lot of time in
> the houses of the red-light district, so that people began to
> call the district Hooker's Division. And from that it came
> about naturally to call the girls that worked the place
> hookers.

Visitors brought a lot of music to The Swamp from their
native parts. There was the popular song "Juba." Slaves went

wassailing around a barrel of persimmon beer to banjo music
and gave the "Juba" handclap and chanted:

> *Juba up and Juba down*
> *Juba all around de town,*
> *Juba dis and Juba dat,*
> *Juba 'round de 'simmon vat!*

In the swamplands yard women recommended ground 'simmon
sprouts as a poultice for pains, boils, and sores. In the hills
folks said persimmon had remarkable properties to foretell the
future. "Cut open a persimmon seed in autumn and examine
the leaf that's between the two halves of the seed. A spoon-
shaped leaf is a warm summer and full crops. If the leaf is the
shape of a knife and fork, watch out. Bad weather and crop
failures ahead."

The cow pokes and steer hands would drift in from Texas—
they were little more than hired hands on horseback in those
days and not yet glamorized as cowboy heroes. The writer,
O. Henry, some New Orleans people claim, used to come with
the cowboys out on a tear after a season of herding and brand-
ing and shipping. There was also horse thieving, a hanging
matter if caught by a posse outside the law. As one state
put it:

> *Horse stealing. Whoever feloniously takes or steals any*
> *horse, mule, or ass, shall be imprisoned in the penitentiary*
> *not less than three nor more than twenty years. The words*
> *"horse," "mule," "ass," shall include animals of both sexes*
> *and all ages.*

The cowboys were attracted to the Sure Enuf Hotel where

they kicked their boots against the bar and sang:

> *I woke up in the morning on the old Chisholm Trail,*
> *Rope in my hand and a cow by the tail.*
> *Feet in the stirrups and seat in the saddle,*
> *I hung and rattled with them longhorn cattle.*

When in trouble with the law and dragged off to the lockup, they'd sober up in the hoosegow and rattle the bars with:

> *Oh, give me a jail where I can get bail,*
> *If under the shining sun,*
> *I'll wake with the dawn, I'll chase the wild fawn,*
> *I'll ride with my saddle and gun.*

The Sure Enuf was no palace from its description, just a two-story shack run by an evil old biddy, big and wide, called Mother Colby. The bar opened into the street where a tart or hustler would act as pull-in, with offers of joy or gambling to passing men. Behind the bar was the wheel and faro layout and the walled-off office, bedroom, and kitchen of Mother Colby. Beyond that were rooms no bigger than closets, with no doors, just curtains, where the customers could bring their women picked up in the bar or street, at the cost of half a bit (a bit was twelve and a half cents, two bits a quarter). Upstairs were beds for foolish passing strangers; anyone might wake up in the night with a knife held at his throat and someone going through his pockets.

The Sure Enuf Hotel later was owned by a character called Crazy Bill Kraus, who departed in 1855 when a happy guest gave him a money belt to put on and hold for him. It was filled with gunpowder and the joker lit the fuse to the explosion that removed the owner to a better or worse place.

The Swamp never really died. Girod Street and Magazine Street continued to exist in their evil ways nearly till the 1890's. The cowboys, cleaned out, went back to the range to get another six months' hard work and a fresh stake for another attack on New Orleans.

> *Bacon in the pan,*
> *Coffee in the pot!*
> *Come up an' get it—*
> *Get it while it's hot!*

When Fulton's Folly on the Hudson turned into a real steamboat, the Mississippi became a highway that moved, and soon the early steamboats gave way to better ones. The first was called, naturally, the *New Orleans*. She left Pittsburgh for a voyage down the Ohio and Mississippi Rivers to New Orleans in January 1812. Later she sank as a boiler exploded after trips between Natchez and New Orleans. Her top speed upstream was two miles an hour better than keelboat. Three other river boats came: *Comet, Vesuvius,* and *Enterprise.* By 1834 there were 230 steamboats in the Mississippi River trade and they soon increased to 450. Between New Orleans and the falls of the Ohio at Louisville the *Enterprise* made the trip in twenty-five days, twenty-three hours, sixteen minutes. Later the *Diana* received five hundred dollars in gold which the Post Office Department had offered to the first boat running New Orleans to Louisville in less than six days. In 1858 *A. L. Shotwell* established four days, nine hours, and nineteen minutes. The time between New Orleans and Natchez was ten hours, thirty-six

Riverfront Saloon

minutes, and forty-seven seconds for the *Robert E. Lee* in 1870. From the start gamblers and whores worked the boats—often splitting with the captains and the pursers.

Mark Twain, who was a river pilot before the Civil War, knew the wild river days and New Orleans nights well. But when writing of his memories and experiences he avoids mentioning the sexual promiscuity on the Mississippi. The restrictons on a writer in his day were such that fornication hardly existed in his books. Though the sporting house and steamboat whores with whom Twain is said to have had a more than passing interest in his youth, and his pornographic story *"Table Talk of Queen Elizabeth"* shows he was a horny man, none of this appears in his texts.

A German traveler on the early boats describes the ladies' cabins and other features:

> They are elegantly fitted up. The windows are ornamented with white curtains, and the beds, twenty in number, with red bombazette curtains and fringes and mosquito bars, besides sofas, chairs, looking glasses, etc. An elegant carpet ornaments the floor. Above deck is an elegant roundhouse, 42 feet in length, 28 in breadth, for the gentlemen. For the convenience of the passengers this room is provided with 26 berths in 13 staterooms, mattresses of Spanish moss (in which the woods of Louisiana abound). Other necessary bedclothes are handsomely flowered. Each berth has a window. Sofas or settees, chairs, two large tables, large gilt framed looking-glasses, several elegantly finished recommendation cards and the regulations of the boat in gilt frames—and finally an elegant carpet adorn the quarters. The climate is exceptionally hot and would scarcely be endurable on board a steamboat in the summer months. The heat of the fire and the boilers would be

Party Music

sufficient to prevent persons from traveling, or would render them uncomfortable while traveling, so the boat is completely covered with awning and above the round-house is an elegantly decorated walk with iron railings and nettings ... there the gentlemen passengers sit comfortably and have a commanding view over the boat, river, and land, and enjoy the cool breeze. The sight of these swimming volcanoes on water is very agreeable. They generally have colors at their poop and the American eagle and stars give a very handsome effect. ...

If Mark Twain and other writers left out any notice of the common sexplay of these river days, the steamboat company didn't. It posted regulations as to the conduct of the men and the women passengers. It appears that the lady had to make the first pass under certain conditions:

No gentleman passenger shall descend the stairs leading to, or enter the lady's cabin unless with the permission of all the ladies, to be obtained through the Captain, under the penalty of two dollars for each offense. ...

No gentleman shall lie down in a berth with his shoes or boots on under penalty of one dollar for each offense. ...

Cards and games of every description are prohibited in the cabin after ten o'clock at night. ...

At noon, every day, three persons to be chosen by a majority of the passengers shall form a court to determine on all penalties incurred, and the amount collected shall be expended in wine for the whole company after dinner.

It is particularly requested that gentlemen will not spit on the cabin floors as boxes are provided for that purpose.

Nobody paid too much attention to all this. The same observer added:

Passage upstream cost $16 to Baton Rouge, $30 to Natchez: downstream the cost was $11 to Baton Rouge,

Big Game.

*$15 to New Orleans. The twenty persons who comprised
the crew of the boat got $9,720 a year in wages, including
the captain's salary, $2,500. Maintenance is very costly in
this part of the country. Everything, especially provisions
are high. One pays from $20 to $45 per month for board in
New Orleans. The expenses in case of damage to machinery, which occur, no one can state. The final and total
expenses are very great. The income obtained is propor-
tionately great. The captain told me that on one trip from
New Orleans to Natchez the income amounted to no less
than $4,000. There is no business in any part of the globe
which is more lucrative than this, but will not be so in a
few years for I know the enterprise of the Americans, and
the rivers as far as they may be navigable will be crowded
with steamboats, and their enterprise will be slackened in
the course of time.*

Soon came the floating palaces, paddle-wheels in the waters of the Mississippi: berths equipped with featherbed and pillows filled with down; rugs and carpets on the floors of the cabins and saloons, plush furnishings. Each gentleman had his own spittoon, gilt and ornamented. "The saloons extend the length of the vessel," says a guidebook, "handsomely fitted up as elegant carpets, magnificent furniture, and grand pianos can make them. The company on the steamboat live as if in a floating hotel, with all the pleasures and enjoyments of hotel life."

Slaves in livery played polite music on the decks or salons of the bigger boats, the piano white and usually heavy with gold. Even on the smaller boats there were usually a few musicians, and if not, some of the crew could pluck a banjo, scrape a fiddle, toot a horn, carry a tune.

> *Hush, hush, somebody callin' my name,*
> *Oh my Lord, oh my Lord,*
> *What shall I do . . .*
> *I'm glad trouble don't last*
> *I'm so glad . . .*

That would do for the churchly minded. But the ladies and the gentry wanted something a bit more lively, and the boys from New Orleans had it:

> *I guess we'll marry in a week,*
> *A week, a week.*
> *I guess we'll marry in a week,*
> *That is, if the weather be good.*
>
> *How're you gonna come to the wedding,*
> *The wedding, the wedding?*
> *How're you gonna come to the wedding,*
> *Dear old buffalo boy?*

Jazz Men

The comic "coon" songs didn't come till later. But comedy was there in an old Overland Trail song carried to the gold fields:

> Light she was, and like a fairy,
> And her shoes were number nine,
> Herring boxes without topses,
> Sandals were for Clementine:
>
> Oh my darling, oh my darling,
> Oh my darling Clementine,
> You are lost and gone forever,
> Dreadful sorry, Clementine.

For themselves the boat Negroes sang music a little more ribald. It wasn't jazz yet, but it pointed to ragtime, and eventually it would take on the new boat to appear around 1900:

> The last time I saw darlin' Corey,
> She had a wine glass in her hand.
> She was drinkin' sweet pizen likker,
> With a low-down gamblin' man.
>
> Don't you hear them bluebirds a-singin'?
> Don't you hear that mournful sound?
> They're preachin' Corey's funeral
> In the lonesome graveyard ground.

And perhaps even an early version of a honky-tonk, barrelhouse favorite:

> Baby, see the spider climbin' up the wall
> He's goin' up there
> To get his ashes hauled . . .

It wasn't easy for the Negro as slave and even as a so-called free man to break free of the vice and sin, the smell and reek of the sporting houses, dance halls, and dives. If he could make music, there was the slim chance he might get a job on one of the boats, and then he'd be adrift in a new world and see things in a new way. One who did just that was Louis Armstrong, and the way he remembered it and talked about it was the way it must have felt to many of the early musicians:

> Dixie Bell *was moving along in almost pitch dark, paddles making a soft chunkling sound. I could see a few stars high up overhead. I found my old corner and sat down. Above the beat of the paddles, everything was still. The shore seemed a long way off. I could just make it out, going past very slow, like a black wall.*

He was going away, and he wasn't sure he'd be welcome. Some day he'd join the others up there in Chicago, and play with King Oliver, another New Orleans boy who had made the trip. It wasn't easy to be comfortable about it:

> *Pretty soon I began to feel alone, and looked round me, nothing but the darkness and steady plunk, plunk of the wheels. I felt far off and not there where I was. I put my hands down on the deck and let them run over the planks to feel them under me. After a little while I got quiet and took comfort out of the stillness, and didn't mind being alone.*

Coming down river seemed more fun for visitors, seeing New Orleans behind the levees, the spires of the churches and the wedges of shack boats selling bait and whiskey and gambling, the shore lined with waiting carriages, the hotel porters smiling, and here and there a steerer for a gambling house, and a few ladies in silk and sunshades. Or were they ladies?

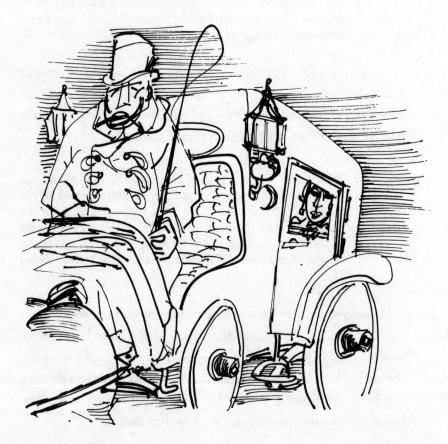

To The Ball

Chapter 6

The Quadroon Balls

One of the excitements of the town were the Bals du Cordon Bleu, which came to be known as the Quadroon Balls. They were actually flesh markets where beautiful girls with some small part Negro blood, often nearly white, came to be met, looked over, appraised for bed, and priced. There was a snobbery, a pecking order among the Negroes. Those with a high portion of white blood were called *gens de couleur*. It was a caste system as rigid as the bigotry of Pasadena. The leaders were the *gens de couleur libres* (free Negroes) and their main interest to sporting house history is that they often produced very beautiful, voluptuous daughters. Since early days the whites had felt the lack of white women, and that lack had produced mulattos in the slave pens at an amazing pace. These ten generations of chicks were now coming home to roost *and* bargain. *Griffes*, the result of the mating of a mulatto and a Negro stood high on the score sheet. Even higher were quadroons, who had a teaspoon more of white genes. They made trouble and Governor Miro had to issue a stern warning.

> *The free women of color in idleness resulting from their dependence for a livelihood on incontinence and libertinism will not be tolerated. They will employ themselves in honest labor or be sent out of the colony. Any excessive attention to dress will be considered as evidence of misconduct.*

The most striking quadroons lived on Rampart Street in little white houses, and while many were not professional prostitutes, their dreams were of a rich white lover whose mistress they would become in style and comfort. Having a nest with one of them was called "hiding out on the Ramparts." It could hardly be called a scandal, for the habit was too popular in New Orleans.

A traveling British author, a lady, wrote of the situation:

> *The connection between white men and quadroons is all but universal. They have been brought up by their mothers to be what they have been; the mistresses of white gentlemen. The boys of some of them are sent off to France or placed on land in the back of the state. . . . They marry women of a somewhat darker color than their own; the women of their own color objecting to them; "Ils sont si degoutants!"*
>
> *The girls are highly educated, externally, and are, probably, as beautiful and accomplished a set of women as can be found. Every young man selects one early, and establishes her in one of those pretty and peculiar houses, whole*

rows of which may be seen in the Ramparts. The connection now and then lasts for life; usually for several years. In the latter case, when the time comes for the gentleman to take a white wife, the dreadful news reaches his quadroon partner, either by letter entitling her to call the house and furniture her own, or by the newspaper which announces the marriage. The quadroon women are rarely known to form a second connection. Some men continue the connection after marriage. Every quadroon woman believes that her partner will prove an exception to the rule of desertion. Every white lady believes her husband has been an exception to the rule of seduction.

What the English lady does not state is that the girls were also carefully trained in the physical side of sexual play and byplay, introducing games that were called "French" by the American innocent. When there were demands for whips, fetishes of hair, of shoe, and other sadist delights from Paris, Rome, or London, these girls could produce an exotic effect— so states a learned old gentleman, Mr. J. R., who was once young and kept a girl on Rampart Street, "the equal of any depraved *connu* in Europe in the art of *fickend*."

The quadroon balls, needless to say, were attended by white men without their wives and daughters. It was little more than high-grade pimping and soliciting, for all the color and candlelight, fine wines and romantic music. One had to have social standing *and* a large income to be invited to meet the girls. There were eight to a dozen balls a month. The gentlemen paid two dollars to get in, and the rest was up to him. The actual ball was dull, polite, with no orgying on the premises. Legend says a great many duels were fought by the gentlemen as the result of insults offered their mistresses, some of whom were wildly depraved.

On The Ramparts

I was comin' down Canal Street
Comin' down Main
Looking for the woman
That uses cocaine.

The Civil War saw the end of these strange mating balls. The city was growing, the rich young men were ruined or dead at Gettysburg or Cold Harbor. The girls mostly had to marry Negroes, much against their wishes. They still flirted with the white men, as is proved by the police records of a half dozen high yellows murdered by black husbands. Some historians think that most of the ladies went north when the Union troops left, and slyly passed themselves across the color line into white society, for they were great beauties. Their descendants today work hard to keep their neighborhoods segregated.

The Orleans Ballroom, where the quadroon fetes had been held, passed ironically to an order of Negro nuns, the Sisters of the Holy Order, who in their pious primness set a slab on the grand staircase where so much body powder, silk, and gay laughter had once filled the place under flaring bayberry candles. It read: I HAVE CHOSEN RATHER TO BE AN ABJECT IN THE HOUSE OF THE LORD THAN TO DWELL IN THE TEMPLE WITH THE SINNERS.

They are gone now, the mulattos and quadroons who were the well-trained, saucy, dexterous women of the Ramparts. But the quadroon of lower rank is still in New Orleans, still often working at the old trade. Only now she is a B-Girl, or a callgirl, under a protector of the Mafia syndicate. She is located in dimly lit apartments in the Garden Section or the Vieux Carré, or often in certain ranch-style motels on the roads leading to the city, across the river or by the lake. In capri pants and fuzzy cashmere sweater, hair dyed red, fingernails silver daggers, the record player producing cool progressive jazz, waiting for the mark to show up for his fun, she turns two or three tricks a busy night. Her commodity, described by a poet as "a sword-cut in water," is still in demand. She has outlived the balls, the cribs, the old-fashioned sporting houses. She has kept step with progress where the older forms of vice and sinning have failed to stay with it. Even the plentiful supply of amateurs, the free sharing of the modern erotic revolution, has not displaced her.

> *You're playing in my orchard,*
> *Now don't you see,*
> *If you don't like my peaches,*
> *Stop shaking my tree . . .*

In the high old days of quadroon glamor, under the calm acceptance of vice, the city fought a battle between two rivals: the bodies of the women against the lure of the playing cards. Gambling has as many devotees as the sporting house. Poker, draw or stud, pleased most; there was faro (bucking the tiger), blackjack (twenty-one), old sledge (seven-up), the shell game, three card monte, chuck-a-luck, even ecarte and brag.

The spell of guessing which walnut hull held the little pea (none of them, it was under the little finger of the gambler till he needed it) never failed to take in the yokel, the deck-hand, the small-town sport. Umbrella Jim Miner always gave a free poem with his pitch as he moved the shells around:

Quadroon Glamor

If you have nerve, you may have plenty;
Five draws you ten, and ten draws twenty.
Attention given, I'll show to you,
How Umbrella hides the peek-a-boo.
Select your shell, the one you choose;
If right, you win; if not, you lose;
The game itself is lots of fun.

But the gamblers were themselves victims of other gamblers, and most were oversexed and spent their money on women. Nell Kimball writes in her memoirs:

> *You could say this for the gamblers, they weren't pikers or tin-horns. They usually dropped their wad at the tables or in the sporting houses. Gamblers, and I've known a dozen of the best, lived on the edge of their nerves. Maybe they didn't show it, but I knew when some big dealer had made a killing; he'd come to the house flushed and his fingers jumpy, and he'd take his favorite bit of gism upstairs and if she had a customer, any girl that was handy. He'd go at it, the girl would tell me later, like he was sawing a woman in half. Loving it up hard and long was the way gamblers often calmed down. When times were slack I've had a few who just moved in with a girl and sat around unshaved, smoking cheroots, dealing and redealing a deck, getting into the kip three, four times a day. Come a steamboat full of sports, or some ranchers or studs looking for action, and the gambler he'd be shaved, perfumed and in his best duds and flawed yellow diamonds. The next few days he'd hardly be sleeping, eating or going to the john. Calm, easy, why you'd think he was made of stone. But once the pigeon was plucked or the action went against him, either way he'd be back in the house, trying to drive one of my girls through the mattress. I suppose the doctors they can explain it. For us madames it was good for business.*

The Negroes who weren't beautiful light-skinned girls, or were churchly, went on carrying the bundles, toting the basket, doing all the dirty hard work there was—and loafing a bit too. The Negro had developed methods to break down his master, and he could yak-yak in public and practice his cakewalk and his "yes suh, yes suh!" for the pleased whites. But under it all he remained a burden of sadness that he was to sing out as the blues, and he delighted in pleasure that he was to practice when he could. He also knew the whites lived in dread he'd get arms, band together, cut throats and rape, repaying for all the colored girls forced down on white bedcovers or taken in steamy hurry on a corn-husk pallet or even in an open field.

> *Well Mama she don't 'low me*
> *To fool 'round all night long . . .*
> *I may look like I'm crazy*
> *But I knows right from wrong . . .*

Early laws tried to regulate the habits of the Negroes, keep them from forming into a menace:

> *The Black Code: Slaves belonging to different masters are not to gather in crowds either by day or by night, under the dwelling or on the grounds of one of their masters, and much less on the highways or in secluded places. Slaves who transgress will be whipped, the offenders shall be branded with the mark of the flower de luce, and should there be aggravating circumstances, capital punishment may be applied at the discretion of our judges.*

Another regulation read:

> *We forbid all the inhabitants or citizens of this colony to permit on their plantations, or at their places of residence, or elsewhere, any assembly of Negroes or Negresses, either*

under pretext of dancing, or for any other cause; that is to say, excepting the Negroes whom they may own themselves. We forbid them to allow their slaves to go out of their plantations or premises for similar purposes. We also forbid the town or country Negroes to assemble in the town of New Orleans, or in its vicinity, or elsewhere, under any pretext whatever, under the penalty, for said Negroes, of being imprisoned and whipped.

For decades the slaves had been gathering in Congo or Circus Square once a week to display their finery of colored rags, calico, all kinds of ribbons, the mean, worn cut-down styles of their masters.... Everybody was running under stall awnings buying pies and beer and lemonade and cakes called *mulatto's belly* or *nun's thighs.* The bootlegger was on the outskirts of the crowd peddling some deadly corn pressing or rum made from the dregs of the sugar mills. The girls wore India kerchiefs of all colors, their hair oiled and combed into the Creole *tignon;* the bucks used bear grease if they could get it; the first dekinkers were already on the market. It was wild and it got wilder, for tomorrow was only hard deadly work.

An early guidebook to the city points this out as one of the sights that visitors should not miss:

Circus public square is very noted on account of its being the place where the Congo and other Negroes dance, carouse and debauch on the Sabbath, to the great injury of the morals of the rising generation; it is a foolish custom, that elicits the ridicule of most respectable persons who visit the city; but if it is not considered good policy to abolish the practice entirely, surely they could be ordered to assemble at some place more distant from the houses, by which means the evil would be measurably remedied.

Bass Player

Go'Way from my Door

There is no doubt that the germs of some phases of jazz were seeded here 50 years or more before the music found its first solid forms. Here on Sunday afternoons the notes of a future music were echoed by the dancers:

> *Rich folks worry 'bout trouble*
> *Poor folk worry 'bout health*
> *I don't worry 'bout nuthin'*
> *All I got is my health . . .*

So even if there were new regulations and the police were there to watch and keep order, once the dust rose from naked or shod heels, when the sweat came up good and warm and the the music grew, what did rules matter?

> *Resolved that from the 1st of May to the 31st of August each year, the slaves, provided with a written consent of their master, be permitted to assemble Sundays on the Circus Square for the purpose of dancing from 4 to 6½ o'clock, P.M.*
>
> *Resolved that it shall be the duty of the commissaries of police of the 3rd and 5th wards, of the commanding officer at Post Trèmé and five men of the day police, to watch that no police ordinance be violated during the time allowed to Negroes to dance on Circus Square.*

The fun started with the banging of beef bones on a cask, (the bamboula) and was maintained without a break until sunset. The favorite dance was called Calinda, a variation of voodoo dance, primitive steps of Africa with borrowings from the French *contre-danses*. The movements of the Calinda and the Dance of the Bamboula were very similar, but for the revolutions of the latter. The bucks attached tin strips to ribbons about their ankles, pranced, leaped into the air, stamped, shouted, "Dansez Bamboula! Badoum! Badoum!" The girls' bodies swayed from side to side and chanted. Children too, all the square a solid stamping and swaying to the bones on the cask, the chanting and clanging of metal that dangled from the ankles.

A visitor reported:

> One might by a little imagination take them for a group of baboons. But as these poor wretches are entirely ignorant of anything like civilization (for their masters withold everything from them that in the least might add to the cultivation of their minds) one must not be surprised at their actions. The recreation is at least natural and they are free in comparison with those poor wretches, slaves of their passions. I saw Gildemeister today among the crowd. He told me that three of the Negroes in the group closest to us were formerly kings or chiefs in Congo.

There is no doubt that all this free excitement led to full sexual contact, the fulfillment of excited passions. It also helped build the legend that the Negro is sexually superior to the whites, that the Negro's pleasure in fornication is stronger, wilder, and more rewarding, and that as a dancer and musician he has a natural gift and a sense of rhythm beyond the skill of the white performer.

None of this seems to be borne out by modern scientific research, but it is part of a legend of the American Negro that was created to make him seem different from the rest of the population.

Fight Night

Sex and erotic play was about the Negro's only form of game and amusement. He could not usually read or write, he had no organized sports, just hard work, and no effort was made to give any other interest beyond some little churchgoing and over-fancy preaching. The *Green Pastures* Negro is as much of a libel as the bull stallion. The Negro child, neglected and on his own, began early to masturbate, often incessantly, as a caged primate will. Both boys and girls usually were clad in one flimsy baglike garment and soon fell into erotic play and mutual satisfaction. Probably, if they had been given games or recreation of other sorts, the average sexual play among them would have been no higher than among white children, if ethnological surveys are correct.

Negroes deprived of companionship of girls or women often coupled with farm animals, and there was a homosexual trend among barracked slaves. But mostly plantation and city life permitted the intercourse of the sexes at odd moments. Marriage was not encouraged, and the use of the males for breeding of more slaves was all the virtue many owners desired.

Negro girls seldom remained virgins much beyond puberty. The pretty ones went to the white master and his sons, over-seers, and retainers. The rest were debauched by other slaves, poor-white rowdies, or boys in the first drive of their glands, who accommodated themselves to anything at hand.

Drink was not easy to get for the Negro. Even dancing and singing and playing of music was banned at times, or confined to stated periods, if permitted at all. No wonder the Negro was so involved with sex and got an undeserved erotic reputation.

Club Date

Trio

As for the Negro's skill as a dancer and music-maker—this is now accepted as an environmental factor rather than a scientific truth. The Negro of talent could not easily become a painter or writer, lawyer or doctor, and certainly, speaking on a much lower talent level, a senator. He had to use what was at hand and what kept him from full boredom. It cost nothing, and felt good, to shuffle and whirl around. It cost little more for a gourd banjo, a set of beef bones, or a home-made drum. Channeled into these two available outlets, music and dance, naturally those talents would develop skills beyond those of people who had multiple forms of entertainment or other ways of making a living.

The best proof of all this is prizefighting. At the turn of the century it was the poor Irish boys like John L. Sullivan who found their only outlet from poverty in the prize ring. But with the Irish skill at ward-heeling and contracting and organizing a sly attachment to the democratic spoils system, the Irish gradually stopped going into the ring in such vast numbers. The Jews, with second-generation ghetto boys like Benny Leonard, King Livitsky, Barney Ross, became the ring heroes. They were followed by the Italians. Today what is left of boxing is dominated by Negro musclemen, driving for one of the few escape hatches into fame and money open to them. Who's next?

BOOK THREE

THE HOUSES

Liberty Hall

Chapter 7

Love love love makes you walk on air
Somebody touch your shoulder
You turn around
Aint nobody there . . .

Voodoo and
Southern Hospitality

The Sunday dances of the Negroes in Circus or Congo Square stopped after the Civil War. In 1880 Negroes who had been slaves frequently came on Sunday to the backyard of an empty property on Dumaine Street where they did the Bamboula and other dances. The *New York World* covered one such event:

> *At this dance a dry-goods box and a pork barrel formed the orchestra. These were beaten with sticks or bones used like drumsticks so as to keep up a continuous rattle, while some old men and women chanted a song that appeared to me to be purely African in its many vowelled syllabification. . . . Owing to the noise I could not even attempt to*

129

*catch the words. I asked several old women to recite them
to me, but they only laughed and shook their heads. In
their patois they told me: "No use, you could never understand it. C'est le Congo!—it is the Congo!" The dance was
certainly peculiar, and I observed that only a few old persons, who had probably all been slaves, knew how to dance
it. The women did not move their feet from the ground.
They only writhed their bodies and swayed in undulatory
motions from ankles to waist. . . . The men leaped and per-
formed feats of gymnastic dancing which reminded me of
some steps in the* jota Aragonesa. *Small bells were attached
to their ankles. "Vous ne comprenez pas cette danse la?"
an old woman asked me. I did not altogether understand
it, but it appeared to be more or less lascivious as I saw it.
I offered the woman some money to recite the words of
the Congo song. She consulted with another and both went
off shaking their heads.*

Up until nearly the twentieth century voodoo or black magic
was powerful in New Orleans and the voodoo queens were the
feared and respected rulers of the black population that came
under their spell. They sold charms, magic amulets, love powders; they pronounced incantations and could cure or curse or
put the evil eye on anyone. And it was rumored they also had
a sideline of strong and nasty poisons. Their powders have
come down to us today under such titles as Big John the Con-
queror, Goofer Dust, and Man Root (to extend the penis).
Modern medicine hasn't studied them too well, but they contain
human hair, fingernail fragments, dried semen, powdered bones
("stole from a hanged man's grave"), and various parts of liz-
ards, bats, and other filth.

Sexual needs and driving desires were attended to by special
mixtures. The local whores used them on their sweet daddys,
fancy men and pimps—for actually most prostitutes are starved

130

for affection, hardly wanting or seldom giving the real thing to their customers.

The most dreaded voodoo item was the *gris-gris*, using the above gruesome items in a leather bag with red and yellow powders well mixed with cayenne pepper. Left on a madame's doorstep by a customer, or tossed-out whore, it could bring disaster to the place—unless, of course, the madame ordered a counter *gris-gris* from the same pre-Freudian witch doctor to fight the first potion.

Voodoo was frankly sexual and depraved. A police officer, Captain Mazaret, reported a raid on the house of Don Pedros, a famous voodoo medic, in which were caught a dozen white women and as many Negro men, the former naked except for thin slips, and all sexually involved under the direction of the doctor. Arrested and fined, Don Pedro said that they were "undergoing treatment for rheumatism." The next day the husband of one of the white women committed suicide in shame at the public exposure of his wife's games.

The sacred virtue of southern womanhood wasn't all it was cracked up to be, or so it would seem. An eyewitness account by a white person who was taken to one orgy by a slave woman records a meeting conducted by the voodoo queen Sanita Dede, a free woman from Santo Domingo:

> *An entrance door was opened at the call of Dede. The first thing which struck me as we entered was a built-up square of bricks at the upper and lower end of the shed, on each of which was burning a fierce fire, casting a lurid light over*

Goodbye

the scene. Along the four sides of the parallelogram of the building were sconces with lighted dips placed at equal distances, which barely added to the dim light of the two pyres. . . . Each man and woman had a white kerchief tied around the forehead, though the heads of the latter were covered by the traditional Madras handkerchief with its five, nay its seven artistic points, upturned to heaven. In a litle while the company, some sixty in all, had assembled. There were males and females, old and young, Negroes and Negresses—handsome mulatresses and quadroons. With them half a dozen white men and two white women. . . .

Near where I stood was an oblong table about eight feet in length and four in width. On its right end stood a black cat, and on its left a white one. I thought them alive, and having a certain fondness for cats, stretched out my hand to stroke the nearest. The touch, that most philosophical of all the senses, soon satisfied me that they were fine specimens of Negro taxidermy. In the center of the table there was a cypress sapling, some four feet in height, planted in the center of a firkin or keg. Immediately behind the cypress and towering above it was a black doll with a dress variegated by cabalistic signs and emblems, and a necklace of the vertabrae of snakes around her neck, from which depended an alligator's fang encased in silver.

At the side of this table I recognized an old Negro by the name of Zozo, well known in New Orleans as a vender of palmetto and sassafrass roots. He seemed to be the corypheus of these unhallowed rites, for the signal for the beginning of the work came from him. He was astride of a cylinder made of thin cypress staves hooped with brass and headed by a sheepskin. With two sticks he droned away a monotonous ra-ta-ta, ra-ra-ta-ta, while on his left sat a Negro on a low stool, who with two sheep shank bones, and a Negress with the leg bones of a turkey, beat an accompaniment on the sides of the cylinder. It was a queer second to this satanic discord. Some two feet from these arch-musicians squatted a young Negro vigorously twirling a long calabash. It was made of one of our Louisiana gourds, a foot and a half long, and filled with pebbles.

133

At a given signal the four initiates formed a crescent before Dede, who was evidently the high priestess. . . .

As the guests stood on the floor (a hardened surface of brick dust) Zozo, leaving his tam-tam, went up to the altar and again drew forth the snake. He forced it to writhe and wriggle over and around the company, uttering the words which were repeated by sixty voices, "Voudou! Voudou Magnian!" He then twirled the snake around his head and dexterously cast it into the blazing pile. Such a yell as arose no words can describe. The rude instruments took up their discords, mixed with yells. Then came a general call for the dance, and no dance of the witches in the Hartzberg ever came up to it. Up sprang a magnificent specimen of human flesh—Ajona, a lithe, tall, black woman, with a body waving and undulating like Zozo's snake—a perfect Semiramis from the jungles of Africa. Confining herself to a spot not more than two feet in space, she began to sway on one and the other side. Gradually the undulating motion was imparted to her body from the ankles to the hips. Then she tore the white handkerchief from her forehead. This was a signal, for the whole assembly sprang forward and entered the dance. The beat of the drum, the thrum of the banjo, swelled louder and louder. Under the passion of the hour the women tore off their garments, and entirely nude, went on dancing—no, not dancing, but wriggling like snakes. Above all the noise rose the voice of Zozo:

> *Houm! Dance Calinda!*
> *Voudou! Magnian!*
> *Aie! Aie!*
> *Dance Calinda!*

The orgies were becoming frightful. Suddenly the candles flared up and went out, leaving nothing but a faint glow from the dying pyres. I had grown sick from heat, and an indescribable horror took possession of me. With one bound I was out of the shed, and with all speed traversed the yard. I found the gate open, and I was in the street and near home sooner than I can tell.

the old school, the eyewitness gives us
report by a French engineer, R. D., of
in the 1920's is clearer and concludes

*avities of mixed whites and Negroes were
exual intercourse in all manners was
achieved. Perversions were the rule, and
en present rushed at the Negroes and
in all sorts of ways, neuf-soixant, gama-
te men were not long in pairing off with
en in intimate biting. The smell was fear-
lust, smoldering candles, body odors of
ple, spilled rum. The foul air, used and
sed place, was almost unbreathable. The
, the screams went lower in pitch, the
unting fell away. Exhausted limbs still
rverse positions, bodies shiny with effort,
the candles going out one by one with a*

Nell Kimball's memoirs touch on this only briefly.

> *I didn't much go for the nigger voodoo shows, and when
> a rich spender from up North who had heard of them
> asked me to provide something fancy and would pay the
> freight, I'd get in touch with Mae Malvina and have her
> send in some mixed dancers and let them go at each other
> to the banging of drums, and that always seemed to please
> the trade.*

This of course was not actual and proper voodoo, but more a
brothel circus put on for clients. White people were fascinated
by voodoo sexuality and were often involved in its orgies. This is
proved by the police report on "Doctor" James Alexander,
"Doctor of Voodoo," who had fancy offices and a voodoo den
on Royal Street, and often produced orgies at the whorehouse

of Lou Jackson, a white madame. In 1889, policemen broke into the house in a surprise raid. They found ten Negro men, near naked, on the floor, attending white women, similarly nude, on chairs in a circle about them. Doctor Alexander was prancing in only a blue sash and a pair of drawers made of silk mesh. The press report said:

> *The police were not prepared for so immoral a show, and for a few minutes could only look on in listless apathy. Recovering their self-possession, the officers quickly set about to perform their duty, and in a twinkling the men and women were being carted off to the station for safe keeping. Caught were two seventeen-year-old girls accompanied by a mother. In Recorder's Court all were found guilty of disorderly conduct. Doctor Alexander and Lou Jackson were each fined twenty-five dollars, the others two dollars and a half and given a warning.*

It is of interest to note that when it came to orgying and making money there wasn't (and is not today) any color line in New Orleans. White madames and black witch doctors used each other's houses, contracted for the business like any theater organization. Negro men and white women and white men and Negro girls played and fornicated and experimented in a state and section of the nation where pure southern womanhood and "keep the Negro in his place" was a battle cry as sacred as magnolia blossoms. "In these things," J. R., quoted before, said: "The Negro's place seemed to be between a white woman's legs. White men of all classes had a firm belief that sleeping with a Negress brought about 'a change of luck.' The blacker the woman the better it was assumed were chances for the change. It was often a mere excuse of some shy white man

Storyville Ladies

for going down the line to a house supplied with black girls. Still, I suppose, it was better than rubbing a hunchback's hump —also said to bring luck."

The attraction of white women to black men was not just folklore. It was the misinformation that Negroes were untiring lovers and that their overlarge genitalia was most effective and rewarding.

The excuse by southerners for this sexual race mixing has been that the whites who cavort naked with Negroes are visiting northerners. A search of old police records shows, however, that over 90 per cent of the white women arrested in these raids were citizens of the city or its surrounding country. (Where records have been torn out or disfigured one suspects that the names of wives and daughters of some fine old local families were obliterated.)

Voodoo was succeeded by *hoodoo* for a while, a rank comedown. The so-called modern voodoo is feeble stuff. New Orleans orgies are hardly ever raided today. "That could sure ruin the tourist business."

> *The fox ran till he came to a pen*
> *The ducks and the geese were in,*
> *A couple of you will grease my chin*
> *Before I leave this town-O . . .*

Chapter 8

If your house catches fire
And there's no water around
Throw your trunk out the window
And let the shack burn down . . .

Terror in the Streets

Nothing could stop the growth of the city. Not wars, as proved by General Andrew Jackson and the Battle of New Orleans (which a pre-radio age fought after peace had been declared) or great fires that flushed the poor whores out of their cribs, took the gamblers away from the cards, the Negroes out of their dismal huts. Disease came too, for it was the time of great plagues, and the prostitutes helped spread whatever was going around. Yellow fever and cholera from time to time attacked the city all through the nineteenth century. It came back again and again. Panic broke out, the sporting houses, the dance halls, the honky-tonks taking on the sights of a Roman pleasure city when the volcanic dust begins to fall. Harlots in their shifts rushed to leave the town, others got drunk, broke into the drink stores, they and their men and protectors creating a witches' sabbath. Gamblers packed their gear; some being fatalists stayed to see what the cards would turn, often the black ace, the card of death.

Nell Kimball reports in her memoirs:

> *Talking with old madames who remember the yellow jack comings they all said there were men and women who when they felt they might die threw themselves into fornication, just not able to get enough of it. The hookers were as bad as the customers, and those who couldn't go out of town or weren't permitted to leave, got drunk as pissants and entertained trade with or without payment. Till the madames had to put the whip to them or have the house bully give them a beating so they'd conduct themselves more like they were whores and not somebody giving it away in a doorway. It was a fearful time the madames would tell me over a gin fizz. In the midst of an epidemic the open cathouses could hardly handle the business, men just aching to get their ashes hauled, staying on all night. A lot just living in the houses, feeling if they had to take the deep six [death in a grave] they'd just as leave be found in bed with a whore and doing what a man seems to want more than anything else when he feels Ol' Scratch is at his heels.*
>
> *I know when there was a war scare, like the trouble with Cuba came to a head, there were lines outside the sporting places and the girls did twenty to fifty tricks a night in the low class cribs, and I cut the time we permitted a customer to take up a girl's attention. In 1910, when it looked for trouble in China, gentlemen callers were thick as summer flies in Basin Street. By 1914 it was a good sign for us madames, all that talk of Kaiser Bill and the U-Boat*

At The Ball

Passed Out

*trouble. The young men came round more often and when
we got ourselves into the war it looked like somebody had
just given us a wheelbarrer and a shovel and opened the
mint and said—take up all you can shovel. But then the
blue-noses they stuck their two cents in, and we had to
close up, it being felt that while the boys were old enough
to die in war, they weren't ready yet to show they had
men's parts and wanted to use 'em.*

*There is something crazy about the sex thing between
men and women when things aren't normal. Polite as you
try to make it and neat as you keep your place, and police
your girls not to be sassy or lippy—come fire, war, epidemics, and it's like a mink farm. Don't think it's just the
riff-raff, the sporting gentry or pete men [safe blowers,
aristocrats of the underworld]. The best people in town
come sneaking in at night, or bold as brass through the
front door, often bringing their own brandy and cigars. It
certainly is an itch that doesn't spare any class.*

In 1832, one of the first cholera epidemics reduced the population from 80,000 to 35,000. In June 1833 the yellow fever
came in and by September 4,000 persons had died. The Reverend Theodore Clapp, a Presbyterian clergyman who lived
through twenty epidemics left a picture of events:

*During the ten succeeding days, reckoning from October
27th to November 6th, all the physicians judged that at
the lowest computation there were five thousand deaths—
an average of five hundred every day. Many died of whom
no account was rendered. A great number of bodies, with
bricks and stones tied to the feet, were thrown into the
river. Many were privately interred in gardens and en-
closures on the grounds where they expired, [their] names
were not recorded in the bills of mortality. Often I was
kept in the burying ground for hours in succession by the*

143

incessant, unintermitting arrival of corpses, over whom I was requested to perform a short service. One day I did not leave the cemetery until nine o'clock at night; the last interments were made by candle light. I found at the graveyard a large pile of corpses without coffins, in horizontal layers, one above the other, like corded wood. I was told that there were more than one hundred bodies deposited there. They had been brought by unknown persons, at different hours since nine o'clock the evening previous. Large trenches were dug into which these uncoffined corpses were thrown indiscriminately. The same day a private hospital was found deserted; the physicians, nurses and attendants were all dead, or had run away. Not a living person was in it. The wards were filled with putrid bodies which, by order of the Mayor, were piled in an adjacent yard and burned, and their ashes scattered to the winds. Could a wiser disposition have been made of them?

Many persons, even of fortune and popularity, died in their beds without aid, unnoticed and unknown, and lay there for days unburied. In almost every house might be seen the sick, the dying, and the dead, in the same room. There were no means, no instruments for carrying on the ordinary affairs of business; for all the drays, carts, carriages, hand and common wheelbarrows, as well as hearses, were employed in the transportation of corpses, instead of cotton, sugar and passengers. One family of nine persons supped together in perfect health; at the expiration of the next twenty-four hours, eight of the nine were dead. Persons were found dead all along the streets, particularly early in the mornings.

Nature seemed to sympathize in the dreadful spectacle of human woe. A thick, dark atmosphere hung over us like a mighty funeral shroud. All was still. Neither sun, nor moon, nor stars shed their blessed light. Not a breath of air moved. A hunter who lived on the Bayou St. John assured me that during the cholera he killed no game. Not a bird was seen winging in the sky. Artificial causes of terror were superadded to the gloom which covered the heavens. The burning of tar and pitch at every corner; the firing of cannon, by order of the city authorities, along all the streets; and the frequent conflagrations which actually occurred at that dreadful period—all these conspired to add a sublimity and horror to the tremendous scene. Our wise men hoped by the combustion of tar and gunpowder to purify the atmosphere.

The cholera had been raging with unabated fury for fourteen days. It seemed as if the city was destined to be emptied of its inhabitants. During this time, as before stated, a thick, dark, sultry atmosphere filled our city. Everyone complained of a difficulty in breathing which he never before experienced. The heavens were as stagnant as the mantled pool of death. There were no breezes. At the close of the fourteenth day, about eight o'clock in the evening, a smart storm, something like a tornado, came from the northwest, accompanied by peals of thunder and terrific lightnings. Morning shone forth all bright and beautiful. The plague was stayed. In the opinion of all the medical gentlemen who were on the spot, that change of weather terminated the epidemic. . . .

There is no record of prostitutes and madames lost in the plague.

Since men first carved their history on stone, they have wondered, marveled, and, oddly enough, cursed the sexual drive:

If any woman, having no husband, has opened her house to the passions of everybody, openly established herself in the way of life of a harlot, and been accustomed to frequent banquets of men to whom she is not related; if she does so in the city, in country-houses, and in that most frequented place, if by her gait, her style of dress, and the people who are seen attending her, by the eager glances of her eyes and the freedom of her conversation, by embracing men, by kissing them, at water-parties and sailing-parties and banquets . . . if in all this she behaves so as to seem a very wanton and lascivious harlot, I ask you whether a young man who has been with her is to be called an "adulterer"—or a lover?

145

So wrote the great Roman Cicero, perhaps after some plague that attacked Rome. The moralists after each epidemic preached against the sporting houses. But landlords, many of whom were respectable—Nell Kimball writes "in some cases the houses were owned by churches"—could not destroy their valuable investment in sporting neighborhoods. Economics usually won out over fear of divine punishment by plague, and human desire for sexual congress was the victor over guilt and the sense of sin.

The reopening of a house was a gala affair with champagne, Negro musicians, often in redcoats, playing away, the girls in new lace and feathers, in frilly peignoirs, the parlors gay with laughter over old jokes, and the faithful customers happy to be alive and kicking and able to prove it, upstairs.

The protection was strong and effective. From the policeman on the beat who had his orders and mooched a free meal and a snort of bourbon in the brothel kitchen, to the local police courts, up to the city hall, and even the state legislature. The sporting houses had friends into whose hands came some of the gold coins and green bills the madames paid for the honor of staying open and active.

There was opposition to the whores and madames, to the horrors of harlotry. The ruin of sons and fathers was pointed out, and even old texts quoted, but it did little to deplete the oldest trade or bother the newest girl in town.

> *Give her my goodbye, her and all her lovers,*
> *Whom she hugs so close to her in their hundreds,*
> *Loving not one, yet with her constant lusting*
> *Leaving their loins limp.*

Brass Group

Things were politically rough all the time. There were rowdy groups that were formed to put men in office or just to riot in favor of their special political bias. Most powerful as trouble-makers were the native Americans, connected with those proud enough of their ignorance to call themselves the Know-Nothing Party. (Such "proud Americans" still exist among the sheriffs, the Pure White Councils, native hate mongers in the Klans, Birchers, and other minority baiters).

The sporting houses were headquarters for many of these street gangs ready to shout for a candidate, rob a store, gang rape, even kill if roused. The whores were pleased to have such wild lovers, and again the madames had trouble collecting fees. This meeting of roughs, political fat cats, hoodlums, pimps, harlots, gamblers, and street thieves caused an outraged cry and a quoting of old preachments against the horror of the whore among us:

> The groundwork of this corporeal beauty is nothing else but phlegm and blood and tumor and bile, and the fluid of masticated food. . . . If you consider what is stored up inside those beautiful eyes, and that straight nose, and the mouth and cheeks, you will affirm the well-shaped body to be nothing else than a whited sepulchre. . . . Moreover, when you see a rag with any of these things on it, such as phlegm, or spittle, you cannot bear to touch it even with the tips of your fingers, nay you cannot endure looking at it; are you then in a flutter of excitement about the storehouses and repositories of these things?

Even this text by the fourth-century Saint John Chrysostom did little to curb the crime in the streets, and when the native

Americans seized parts of the city, they wrecked the office of the Registrar of Voters. Nothing was left in the drama except to organize the Vigilantes, just as in a western epic on the screen. Several hundred red-blooded sports formed a mob, invaded the Vieux Carré where the whores, some native Americans, were strongest. The Vigilantes seized the Cabildo on Jackson Square, and, having the city jail, they moved next door to the Arsenal on St. Peter Street, where they got guns and powder and ball and even a few ancient cannon that could still fire. The *putsch* was made official by notices in all the papers the next day, and the sporting houses waited to see which side would win before clearing ready for the victors:

> *People of New Orleans: the Vigilantes having resolved to free our city from the murderers who infest it . . . have assumed its temporary government. We call upon all good men and true to join. The Vigilance Committee will inflict prompt and exemplary punishment upon well known and notorious offenders and violators of the rights and privileges of citizens.*

The walls of the city sported a public poster:

> *"To The Citizens of New Orleans." After years of disorder, outrage and unchecked assassination, the people, unable and unwilling either to bow down in unresisting submission to a set of ruffians, or to abandon the city in which their business, their social sympathies, and their affections cluster, have at length risen in their might—have quietly taken possession of the arsenal and buildings at Jackson Square, and have established here the headquarters of a Vigilance Committee; pledging each to the other to maintain the rights unviolable of every peaceful and law-abiding citizen, restore public order, abate crime, and expel or punish, as the law may determine, such notorious robbers and assassins as the arm of the law has, either from*

Father and Son.

the infidelity of its public servants, or the inefficiency of the laws themselves, left unwhipped of justice.

For the present the ordinary machinery of police justice is suspended—the mayor and the recorders, we understand, yielding up the power they confess the inability to exercise for the preservation of public peace, and the preservation of property; and the Vigilance Committee will therefore provisionally act in their stead, administering to each and every malefactor the punishment due his crimes, without heat, prejudice or political bias. All citizens who have sympathies with this movement, and who think the time has come when New Orleans shall be preserved like all other well-ordered and civilized communities, will report themselves without delay at the Principal, where the character of the movement will be explained, and the determination of the people more fully made known. All has been done noiselessly thus far; all will continue noiselessly, dispassionately, and justly, but the ruffians who have dyed our streets in the gore of inoffending citizens, and spread terror among the peacable, orderly and well-disposed, must leave or perish. So the people have determined. Vox Populi, vox Dei.

There were days of rioting and a little looting of stores; businesses were closed, and many of the sporting houses put up their shutters, didn't light their red lamps. Yet business in some houses went on as usual and there were rumors of a few being wrecked and girls assaulted, although none of this is published record. After marching around and around a few citizens were beaten up because they were in the wrong part of town, and a cannon exploded and killed a man. Also the Vigilantes killed four of their own men "by mistake." In the end the Vigilantes gave up being the law and over a dozen of the leaders, respectable men of money and power, left by steamboat till the thing blew over. Eleven bodies were found in the trenchs, but the coroner came "to no conclusion except that they were dead."

I'm goin' back to New Orleans,
My race is almost run.
I'm goin' back to spend my life
Beneath that risin' sun.

The whorehouses gave another fete, and celebrated victory or defeat of their steady customers—and New Orleans went on as before. The reformers withdrew to reshape their ranks, the preaching in the churches was against sin—as was expected. And many a pious brother went directly from hearing an edifying sermon to his favorite sporting house to see how the girls were spending Sunday afternoon. Then home to supper—dinner was the name of the midday meal in those days—and evening prayer. The family that prays together stays together.

Actually the sporting houses were the most respectable of the vice and pleasure centers of the town. They did not often descend to the level of the barrelhouses, dance halls, saloons, panel joints, and vulgar entertainments that gave New Orleans a bad reputation. Yet the sporting houses were unfairly lumped with these low criminal elements by people unaware of the power and wealth of the madames, and the landlords, merchants, and property owners who backed them. Prostitution was an economic force. The establishments were investments running into the hundreds of thousands of dollars, and their food, liquor, linens, wine cellars, ornate lighting, even plumbing (in an age in which the Saturday bath in a washtub were still cherished and the two-holer in the yard was an innovation) brought business to the town. The buying power of the madames was extensive and the banks elbowed each other for their accounts.

Class.

Many young men got their first education in elegance from the costly marbles, bronzes, fine rugs, and genuine oil paintings of the brothels. In gaslight and later in the first electric lights they sat on fine furniture modeled for French kings, saw Tiffany glass, rare feathered fans, mother-of-pearl inlayed bedsteads, drapes of silk and velvet not seen at home. The madames imported furniture and art from Europe, India, China, and Japan, and while it was over-ripe and perhaps too rich in red and yellow, the heavy gold frames pictured beauty in landscape and flesh. It was a world that suggested fine living, and it gave many an American on his way to success his first look at what life could hold if he went out to make his pile and gained some share of easy living when he built his own place. "The whorehouse," said J. R., "has never been given enough credit for its great part in forming a taste for architecture and interior decoration in American life."

Nor did the bathed, scented, curled, and touched-up girls harm a man's libido. After even one visit it was harder for a man to accept his placid marriage with a prim, uninformed girl who looked upon lust as a wild animal that she was forced to accept "because God and the law said so." But one didn't have to act up to enjoying it too much. The sexual erotic revolution was too long delayed in America, and so it prolonged the life of the sporting house for a hundred years.

Few parents in the nineteenth century told their daughters the facts of life, and the wedding night and the deflowering was often brutal and so shocking it ruined many women's lives and, some claim, even filled mad houses. The eternal pregnancies, in an age when to contracept was in a vague way against

God's stern rule to beget and beget, caused many women to detest the sexual act.

The male was no better off in most cases. He had been taught as a child that to show interest in his sexual parts would lead to insanity, soften the brain, taint his future children, bring pimples and the instant horror of hair growing on the palms of his hands!

It is hardly a surprise then that the manners, gaiety, indifference to the terror of punishment, eternal or by society, should relax a man visiting a whorehouse that had his family trade—where sexual pleasuring was frank, joyful, playful, and cost only money.

> Go tell my baby sister:
> "Don't do what your sister done,
> Stay away from that house in New Orleans,
> They call the Rising Sun."

The male was free here of mother, that great all-devouring Mom and her silver cord, perhaps also away from an earnest, serious, often harassed young wife, whose personal physical ailments were always on hand, who never really revealed her naked body for pleasure. (It is amazing to find so many texts in which married people confess they undressed in the dark and never removed their nightshirts when making love.)

In the cathouse a man had no problem of conception, of adding to an already large family; no nagging about bad children, bills, a need for a new horse and buggy; no problem of sassy servants and the leering vulgarity of the iceman or the fishmonger.

Under madame's disciplined eye (and hard hand) the girls were all charm and willing partners, their drawers and laces a delight, the beds wide and overcomfortable, the mirrors worth a look any time, the entire deed done with a partner who by sound, gesture, and technique insisted this male was the boldest, wildest, most endowed, most experienced of her entire career.

Madam and Girl.

Sportin' Line.

Later, in discrete but revealing light, a man could sit dressing and wink at himself in the shameless mirrors, feeling he was the old Adam and proud of it. The sweat of ten generations of whores had been blotted out by carbolic or lysol.

The customer paid for what he got, and, as so many later admitted, they also got a course in manners in the better houses, an ability to face all women in later life on more sophisticated terms than in their own homes. A kind of worldliness was acquired that transcended the town or city they came from.

157

These by no means intangible rewards were not of interest to the moralists who rightly were concerned about maintaining the family, living by God's word, and seeing no pleasures in what they themselves did not need or what they repressed. Nell Kimball noted: "I never met a bluenose yet who didn't want all the dirty details of your trade, and some drooled a bit as they rolled their eyes up at the ceiling. And I've been propositioned to put out by gents who would surprise you. A few, with the hot breath and the wet palm, they were sicker than anybody I ever saw."

She is admittedly a prejudiced witness.

> *Some folks say a preacher won't steal.*
> *I caught two in my cornfield.*
> *One had a bushel; one had four.*
> *If that ain't stealin', I don't know the score.*

Change of Luck

The Fight

Chapter 9

All women are sitting on a fortune,
if they'd only realize it.
                    Basin Street saying

How to Succeed
in the
Sporting House Business

The sporting houses as economic units frowned on the vulgar crime of the rest of the town, and were often blamed for what went on away from the calm, well-run haven of *hommes moyens sensuals*. Streetwalkers with no real base but a room hired by the hour and drinking and gambling halls, all hurt the reputations of the houses that tried to surround mercenary copulation with the proper fittings of civilized ease, comfort, and a sense of *coquetterie*.

The press and travelers, always seeking sensations, wrote gleefully of the crime wave that never ended but came in fresh every year like a booming surf, bringing its contents to spill on the delta: "Murders here are an everyday occurrence and the papers daily give details. A thousand murders might be committed in New Orleans, and if the murderers could not be found on the spot, our authorities would never afterward make any efforts to have them punished.

"The proportion of crime to the population is, to a European, perfectly astounding. (The city) is suffering from a reign of terror, and we sarcastically apologize to Mayor Waterman for calling his attention to the danger which ordinary, peaceable citizens run whenever they venture abroad. It is most true that our city has been infested by a band of desperadoes who have shed innocent blood and spread terror and consternation among certain classes."

On certain low streets were the sporting houses that paid protection money or hired guards, or did both. Crime festered in the Irish Channel district where the "arse bare" Irish settled on St. Thomas Street, Corduroy Alley, Rousseau Street, on the fringe of Sorpaparu market. Factseekers entered at their own risk:

> The inhabitants of the Alley appear for the most part to be an intemperate and bloodthirsty set, who are never contented unless engaged in broils, foreign or domestic, such as the breaking of a stranger's pate or the blacking of a loving spouse's eye. These are the ordinary amusements of the Alley. . . . Honest people doubtless live on

Blues.

House Show

St. Thomas Street, but they must have a hard time of it if they manage to keep their skulls uncracked and their reputations unstained.

We have never observed in any of the dance houses of Gallatin or Barracks Street, or the ballrooms of the demimonde further downtown, the utter abandon which has characterized these places. A hall would be filled with some two or three hundred scowling, black-bearded, red-shirted visitors coming from every port, prison and lazar-house, and presenting such a motley throng as Lafitte or any of the pirates of the Gulf might have gathered for their crews. With a piano and two or three trombones for an orchestra, and with dances so abandoned and reckless that the cancan in comparison seemed maidenly and respectable, one can form an idea of what the scene was.

The sound of the trombones sets us on the trail of the fore-runners of jazz. When the Civil War ended, many Confederate army bands dumped their instruments in New Orleans pawn shops, and Negroes bought the battered music tools cheaply and began to play them with no knowledge of reading music or the proper way to handle the slides or valves. They began to play the popular ragtime in their own way. So the sounds in the night over the howls of the whores, ponces, stick-up artists, thugs, and half-drugged sailors were the first *wha-wha* jackass sounds of jazz not yet fully formed or named. It was but a step up from here to the parlor houses where a man could play his music in better surroundings and be fairly free of the fear of being killed by a bottle in the hand of a drunken merrymaker.

The madames had a way of quieting troublemakers and each had her own strong-arm boy to hold down a heaving, raging customer. "A respectable place," Nell Kimball tells us, "never threw a trouble maker out onto its own front steps. I always had my boys carry the John to some other house's sidewalk."

165

Nell Kimball, according to her memoirs, came to Basin Street in 1880, and under another name opened a first-rate sporting house in a fine old three-story building. She had come from St. Louis where she had spent ten years as a whore in a well-run German speaking establishment, and become involved in a love affair with a cigar manufacturer, whose wife had her run out of town. The cigar maker had given her enough money to travel, and some over, and she settled in New Orleans with introductions to the city hall government and the police.

Properly certified as a "square-shooter" and backed by two town merchants who provided furniture and wines to the brothels, Nell Kimball spent twenty thousands dollars—a vast sum before the inflated money of today—doing the place over before she opened for business with a gala:

> *You can say you never saw better people any place in town. I had put in a lot of Venice glass over the gas jets and drapes of blood-red velvet reaching to the floor and had eight girls I had picked out myself, some from as far as San Francisco, and two high yellows I called Spanish, and nobody gave a damn what they were after they went upstairs for wick dipping.*
>
> *Furnishing a sporting house, and I did over three of them before I retired in 1917, called for some sense and a lot of feeling for the customer's comfort, habits and little tricks. I used only the best food and had a cook, Lacey Belle, who was with me for twenty-two years. She did all the marketing, and two darkies carried home the stuff fresh as she bought it. Lacey Belle could cook French, and she could cook Jim Brady style or American, but I never served any guests poor food or food badly cooked. Girls and gentlemen ate the best. The silver and the dishes were heavy and good. Wine came in dirty bottles with the right labels for the Johns who knew what they wanted. But for*

those who didn't, I had a lot of fancy bottles which we refilled from time to time with red wine and white wine from a Cajun farmer's barrels. Whiskey was the best Kentucky bourbon, and my handyman and coachman, Harry, could mix gin-fizz, tom-collins, horse's necks—all the things some sport called for to show off he'd been to Saratoga or Churchill Downs or Hot Springs.

Linen is a big item, and a house can go busted if that isn't watched, counted, marked, and sent to the best wash-tub mammy in town who had the top whorehouse trade. I always changed linen after every customer, but some houses did it only every day, and the cribs they just had a gray sheet on a pallet and maybe never changed it, just threw it away when nobody would lie down on it.

I never had no truck with the idea whores had hearts of gold, and I never turned a girl down because she was rabbity and jumpy, what they later called neurotic. They made the best whores sometimes. If a madame can't handle girls, she's better out of the business. The girls make or break a house, and they need a solid hand. You had to watch out for Lesbians among them, and while I didn't mind the girls doing a bit of chumming and doubling up, if I found a dildoe, I knew it had gone too far. Girls that become libertines with each other don't satisfy the johns because they are involved with themselves.

I had a lot of girls who were mulatto, what they call metisse, negrillonne, and from Brazil caloclo and mulato. If they couldn't pass as Spanish I'd turn them over to a madame that ran a nigger house. I never ran anything but a white whorehouse with a little color, you might say, for flavor. I was firm but I got no pleasure from making their life mean—as one or two madames did.

I'd punish the girls with fines, and if they got real out of line I'd have Harry work them over, but not bruise them. This may sound mean and cruel, I suppose, but they were often wild girls, a bit batty upstairs, who could do harm if they went off the deep end. And once a house gets a reputation as having girls who don't act right with the customers you might just as well close up and turn out the red light in the front of the place and throw away the key.

Visitors

I paid the girls one third of what they earned and never held back, and I didn't shark them with interest on loans I made them, or get them on drugs or have them mulcted by fancy men like some houses did. I never cottoned to the sweet daddies that attached themselves to a girl's earnings.

The girls got their money and they could do what they wanted with it. They were charged for meals, linen, room, and if they weren't fall-down drunks, I threw in the likker free. A drunk is no good as a whore. You can't hide her breath, and she doesn't do her work in style. Hookers are mean but sentimental. They cry over dogs, kittens, kids, novels, sad songs. I never cared much for a girl who came to work in a house because it was fun for her. There was a screw loose somewheres. I remember a Jew girl from a good family who was the wildest thing in the act ever to hit Basin Street. She lasted two months, tried to kill a John with a chair, and hung herself that night in the attic.

I never knew many whores to hold on to any money. But there was a half Indian girl from Oklahoma who went back and married a farm boy who became a big oil man and later a U.S. congressman.

I always ran a tight house the way a good captain runs a tight ship. Mornings a house was like a tomb. The girls sleeping and Harry hosing down the plant boxes and side-walks, the shutters up. Inside Lacey Belle and two maids were cleaning up the cigar trays, sweeping, dusting, rubbing out the wet glass stains and sorting out the linen. There was no use making any dinner because it wasn't until two o'clock that some of the girls would yell down to the maids to shake their black ass and bring up coffee. The girls were pretty weak stomached till the coffee came. And I had to watch the lushes didn't get any likker.

I insisted everybody be down at four o'clock for supper. And I made them wash, do their hair before they came down, and wear clean robes or peignoirs. I saw they had a good meal. No la-dee-da-ing. A gumbo or okra soup, steak, potatoes, turkey, white meat of chicken, a river catfish fried golden, apple pie and lots of stewed fruit. One of the problems with whores is constipation. I insisted they stay regular and used cascara and rubarb. At first most didn't like the daily bath I made them take, but I didn't put in all that plumbing for just show. And after a while perfume doesn't hide the human being under it. Bidets were new to a lot of them, and one Kansas farm girl used it as foot bath till I took her in hand. Coming from the corn-husk and catalogue belt she had never seen toilet paper either.

I didn't let the girls out much, but each got a day off, and the Catholic whores were usually very pious and went to mass. You could tell when they'd been to confession. They were all wide-eyed and polite and enjoying a state of grace. I didn't let them have crucifixes in their room on the wall. One of our best customers was a very wonderful Jew gentleman who used to send each girl a basketful of wine bottles every Christmas. He later owned a string of movie places and he always sent me a season pass.

Till nine in the evening the girls sat and smoked, did their hair over, lied to each other, bragged, looked over the magazines—they hardly ever read a newspaper till the funnies were popular.

They were always borrowing from each other and in debt to Suroyin, the old Greek bundle peddler who sold them robes, dresses, underwear and shoes against future payment. The girls who had a fancy man had to keep him happy with clothes and gambling money and bail money to get him out of jail for a slashing or a little robbery. I didn't allow the fancy men in the place, but once a month they could come to dinner on a Sunday.

Nine o'clock the three darkies would start the music in the front parlor, and the piano player would be noodling on the baby grand in the back parlor, which was the parlor for the big muckamucks, the city hall boys, the state capitol gents, the better family folk, out-of-town actors. (John Barrymore's father left a top hat I kept around for a year.)

A stray customer would maybe show around ten and ask for a girl. If he looked a bit out of place, I'd say, "I'm sorry, we're closed by a death in the family." The sports didn't start coming in till after a late supper near ten. I'd ring a

Cock Fight

bell for one of the nigger maids to ask some of the girls to come down. I never called out, "Company, girls," or as some did, "Gentleman callers, ladies." I let the maid usher the girls in.

By midnight the place on a good night would have a dozen to twenty men in both parlors, the girls circulating and the maids passing out drinks. I used high class nigger help, and the girls would not jump at being pinched in the derriere or boobs, but beyond that I'd move in and say we catered to gentlemen and I was sure he was one. No one well bred would talk back to that.

Most of the girls were dressed in evening gowns I had approved of. They had the damndest taste for frou-frou and feathers. I didn't allow much piling up of hair with rats or pads unless they had a customer who was all for hair. Some of the girls dressed as jockeys in tight white pants, caps and patent leather boots or as school girls in buckle shoes, big blue hair bows.

I always liked trade that was steady and came back and could find a way to feel at home away from home, you might say. An old client and his visitors were welcome, and any passing prizefighter (white), actor; senator or judge. I didn't care much for just trade off the street, and in good times I discouraged it.

The girls got cold tea in their drinks, but every fifth round I'd give them a belt of rye. Champagne was a bulls-eye for them, and they'd save their corks. They got a dollar a cork. I didn't like loud girls or bold girls. But I always kept a self-starter around, a girl who worked on shy Johns, or adolescents down from college getting their cherry copped. She had to make the advances but not frighten them off. A house that got a rumor going against it as a place where shyness or impotence couldn't be brought round, lost a good part of its special trade.

By two in the morning the rooms were all occupied and I'd be drinking with the waiting customers, and the girls would sort of slide downstairs again, their faces refreshed and their hair combed. I'd make introductions and manage at the same time to get the fee, if I hadn't gotten it in ad-

House Mother

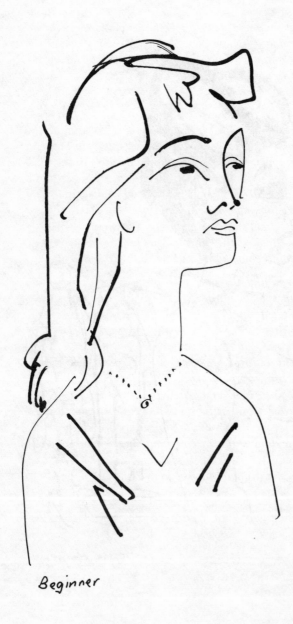

Beginner

vance. And I'd see the departing guest to the door, being sure all likker and breakage was paid for. Some of the old trade I remember, a magistrate, a court judge, used to kiss me on the cheek goodnight and give me a pat on the fanny.

I had a housekeeper—usually an old dyke—and she kept order upstairs and took care of the linens. By three the crowd business was petering off. The all-night tricks, Johns who stayed the night, were tucked away, and on the third floor there might be a show going on, two or three of the girls doing a dance, a bit outré, just enough to set up the clients who could join in as a group or a solo. Unless a special guest asked for a little voodoo, I hardly went in for group orgies.

The girls down in the parlors sat around listening to the piano player finger a cakewalk, or the band do Stephen Foster. Around four o'clock they went up to bed; the most rabbity I gave a hooker of gin. By five unless there was a big all night ball in town, or a special boat was in and people were making the rounds of the town, I had the light turned out downstairs. Harry got the doors locked. I hardly ever opened the door to knocking, and the cop on the beat would come along and tell them to shove off.

I never counted the take till the next day—I was that bushed—but soaked my feet in hot water and one of the maids would rub my neck while I got out of my corset and into bed with a cup of hot milk and nutmeg. I was a poor sleeper as I got older, and sometimes I'd take one of the maids to bed with me and we'd just talk lazy, gab with a night-light burning, talk about the Johns, the family life the maid came from, and when the girl saw I was real woozy she'd get out of bed and I'd cork off and have a sleep until ten or eleven in the morning when I'd hear the girls coming downstairs, or Harry moving around with the big watchdog we kept by the stable, or outside testing shutters, and I'd come awake, and then it was goodbye Charlie to sleep.

Some of the madames sniffed cocaine, but my tensions were usually under control and I'd just lay there—half out —until the morning light came in through the shutters, just a line of light.

I always had plenty to do, getting the police and city hall cut of the take put in envelopes, inspecting the laundry with the housekeeper, the cleaning bills, replacing busted chairs, lamps, linens. The house in the morning was still a bit strong. Body powder, Lysol, dead cigars, the woman smell of it always heavy, and spilled likker. After awhile to me a house wasn't a good house unless it had that musk smell in the morning. Lacey Belle, the cook, and me would drink our coffee in the kitchen, all the girls sleeping, and I'd read the paper and see who was at the good hotels and make bets with Lacey as to who would show up that night.

That's pretty much the average day in any house I ran. And mostly they were good and like that, and not like the whorehouses in the books and plays and later the movies. There never was a real sporting house in any of them, just men's ideas of them, the average John's idea of people they didn't know a goddamn thing about, except the dreams we were supposed to make real for them.

Such is Nell Kimball's picture of a high-class sporting house on Basin Street. She ran her place on a good street, unlike the majority of the wild boisterous places around Canal Street north of St. Charles Avenue and into the Vieux Carre. After the Civil War the carpetbaggers ruined the city and more of the best respectable houses fell to the madames. The town had a population of nearly 200,000 and with the help of the law and the police the vice places were running on Gravier, St. John, Union, Royale, Basin, Conti, Camp, Franklyn, and Perdido.

Nell ran a ten-dollar luxury house, and prices went down from there, till you got to the fifteen-cent, two-bit Negro cribs. Graft, boodle to the proper people, kept them all open and running, and the income was huge. Nell Kimball at no time gives a full account of her income. New Year's and Mardi Gras were big times, and the bite ran high for protection. Nell wrote she paid two hundred and fifty dollars a week for protection. Big payments were made directly to some police officer, but the average brothel payoff in bills and coins was left on the front steps for the cop on the beat to pick up, and a policeman coming in to the stationhouse with pockets filled with silver coins was a common sight.

Free-lance madames and their girls who had no protection were open to arrest. The fine was usually twenty-five dollars for the madame and ten dollars for each girl, and an added word of advice to make a connection.

Some citizens felt it would be best to license prostitution, but that still called for graft to keep from being pulled in for breaking rules. Licensing had been tried in 1857. The Common Council passed Ordinance No. 3267 for lewd and abandoned women: "It shall not be lawful for any woman or girl, notoriously abandoned to lewdness, to occupy any one-story building, or the lower floor of any house within these limits in certain districts. A fine of twenty-five dollars for violation, with penalty of twenty-five dollars for each day after the third the offense went on."

Section Three of the ordinance hoped to bring in revenue of $75,000 to $100,000. A prostitute could live and a madame could operate above the first floor of any building in New Orleans if licenses were obtained. The annual fees cost $100 for a girl and $250 for the keeper. No license meant a fine of $100, half to the informer.

In succeeding sections fines went from $5 to $25 for disturbing the peace, occasioning scandals, drinking in coffee houses. No living in the same house for white and Negro prostitutes and no accosting men from door and windows, nor sitting upon the steps in an indecent posture or strolling about the streets of the city indecently attired.

> *If I had a-listened to what mama said,*
> *I'd be at home today.*
> *But I was young and foolish, poor girl,*
> *I let a gambler lead me astray.*

Wise in the ways of the world, the madames set up a sporting house lobby and got some lawyer-client to go to speak for them. It took a lot of doing, but the courts in time held the license law to be unconstitutional. The madames had the court declare they were to get their money back, money collected by the city from the whorehouses. Perhaps the madames did get some of it back. They were in business as usual again, paying protection as usual and not having to face the insult of being "made to buy a license like a street dog." It took forty years to bring on the next legal prostitution system in New Orleans.

The splendor of the sporting houses' decor attracted attention. Since a respectable lady couldn't go to see the latest drapes, rugs, mirrors—and her husband wouldn't talk—a reporter did the job. We do not know if he was talking about Nell Kimball's place, but it sounds like a top house.

> *He came into a hallway adorned with a couple of statues*
> *representing some obscure divinities of light, and in whose*
> *hands were lighted flambeaux. Beyond this lay the*
> *drawing-room, peopled with a few figures in glittering*
> *attire, and who, from their costumes and manners, might*

178

*have been visitants from the Mountains of the Moon.
Neither did the decorations of the rooms, in the pictures
that hung from the walls, the plated mirrors, the delicately
tinted furniture, appear to be altogether of a sub-lunar
character, though evidently intended to embody a syba-
rite's dream—luxury and repose. The grotesque and bizarre
aspect of everything—splendor without comfort, glitter
and sparkle suggestive of death and decay.*

One of the houses on Basin Street that pioneered in interior
decorating was that of Kate Townsend, a fine place where it
cost twenty-five dollars to stay the night with a breakfast
thrown in and money for a cab if needed. Here one wife did
break in, as told in a letter to the *New Orleans Times:*

> *The lady of an Alderman, who heard that her husband
> visited the house, resolved to see for herself. She disguised
> herself and entered the house, where she found nearly the
> whole city government, with the President of the Board
> of Aldermen or the Mayor—we forget which—at the head
> of the table and her husband at the foot.*
>
> *The opening of another of those "whited sepulchres"
> on Basin Street offers a fitting opportunity of calling the
> attention of the public, and particularly the city authorities
> and the police, to the condition of this fine street. Between
> Canal and Common Streets almost every house is of bad
> repute, lighted up at night with music and revelry within,
> having a constant stream of men going in and out, and the
> late investigation into the homicide that took place reveals
> the scenes that are nightly therein enacted. To such a
> state has the neighborhood come that several of our most
> respectable citizens have had to sell their family mansions
> at half the price they cost to build, and have removed from
> the locality, and others we learn are about to follow, as
> they cannot permit their families longer to remain within
> hearing and seeing of the nightly orgies that are going
> on there.*

The letter was signed "Suffering Property Holder."

Baritone Sax

Competition was strong among the madames for the most interesting place. There was the descendant of the heroine in Longfellow's famous poem, who had an historic painting in her parlor with the gold sign: *Mr. and Mrs. Hiawatha, Ancestors of Minnie Haha.* Minnie had houses on both Union and Basin Streets with hitching blocks of cast-iron Negro boys out front. Kitty Johnson was famous as a madame whose lovers fought a duel for her on her sidewalk, the winner getting a free dinner with the girls.

It was hardly romantic, however, when one comes to Josephine Killeen, where the lure was Mollie Williams and her ten-year-old daughter, available as a team for parties at fifty dollars. The police broke up this early-day Lolita setting, and Mrs. Killeen was outraged that "a girl should be taken from a mother who needed her help." Girls from the ages of twelve to sixteen were often found in the brothels, and the rage of citizens only raised the price for the Humbert Humberts of the day.

Kate Townsend was the madame who gave proper class to Basin Street. Nell Kimball tells us, "she had the largest breasts in New Orleans and it was a fine sight to see her traveling with them before her." Kate was a drinking woman, a power in local politics; and No. 40 Basin has gone down in history as the most ornate luxury sporting house in America. Her own suite she claimed cost her forty thousand dollars to furnish with Arabian carpets, marble fireplaces, and solid walnut paneling. The rumor was that her *boite a l'ordure*—her chamber pot—was solid gold (Nell Kimball claims it was only plated).

A reporter, carried away by the sight of her bedroom, found:

181

a magnificent etagere, upon which were statuettes, the work of renowned artists, and small articles of vertu betraying good taste, both in selection and arrangement. A finely carved small marble table stood next, while adjoining this was a splendid glass door armoire, on the shelves of which were stored a plethora of the finest linen wear and bed clothing. Next to the armoire was a rep and damask sofa, and over the mantel was a costly French mirror with gilt frame. A large sideboard stood in the corner next to a window on the other side of the chimney, and in this was stored a large quantity of silverware. Another armoire similar to the one just described, a table and the bed completed the furniture of the room saving the armchairs of which there were quite a number, covered with rep and damask, with a tete-a-tetes to match. The hangings of the bed, even the mosquito bar, were of lace, and an exquisite basket of flowers hung suspended from the tester of the bed. Around the walls were suspended chaste and costly oil paintings.

He does not name the artists, but most likely there was a Corot, who, a wit once said, had painted three thousand paintings of which five thousand were in America. Many in whorehouses. The entire house cost nearly a hundred and fifty thousand dollars to furnish in a day when money had five times the value it has today.

Kate Townsend kept two dozen girls. The maid always showed the gentlemen to the parlor. Wine cost fifteen dollars a bottle. The girls were told to be polite and not talk sassy unless requested to. The client paid fifteen dollars and, for extra popular girls, twenty. Nell Kimball tells us Kate wasn't above taking a John upstairs herself, and her fee in her palmy days was fifty dollars an hour:

I never myself took any but a few old customers upstairs. I felt it hurt the dignity of a house to have the madame available just to anyone. But Kate, who was usually bottled, would take on anyone. She didn't hold to her high-toned position. A murder was done at her place in 1870, right in front of her with a knife and pistol. She told me later she always kept that knife on hand. She had been taken up by a Treville Sykes, from a good family. When she got too fat to move around much, he moved into the place. She knocked him around a lot in her saw-edge temper, once partly cutting off his nose with the murder knife. She was always looking for young studs and took up with a tinhorn named McLean, who also lorded it in the place. In 1882 or 3 fighting between Sykes and Kate was mean and she always carried the big knife. Sykes killed her with the knife she kept at the house, she taking a dozen fearful wounds and dying hard. She was buried in a six hundred dollar silk dress, laid out fine in her own parlor, champagne for all, and it was good champagne. I had three glasses of it. It was a grand burial, the coffin of bronze cost five hundred dollars alone, and there were two dozen carriages following Kate to Metarie Cemetery. Not a gentleman friend showed up, but she couldn't have expected them. The press had a holiday:

TERRIBLE FATE OF KATE TOWNSEND AT THE HANDS OF TREVILLE SYKES

CARVED TO DEATH! WITH THE INSTRUMENTALITY OF A BOWIE KNIFE

HER BREASTS AND SHOULDERS LITERALLY COVERED WITH STABS

With one foot on the platform,
And the other one on the train.
I'm goin' back to New Orleans
To wear the ball and chain.

Sykes, user of instrumentality, was acquitted on the plea of self-defense, and he even produced a will making him the heir to the brothel and Kate's fortune. It had been set at two hundred thousand dollars, but after lawyers and the court officials had worked on it a few years, it was figured at thirty-three thousand dollars. The lawyers grabbed thirty thousand as fees and a lot went for court costs and "items." The murderer of his sweetheart got thirty-four dollars in the end and a lot of newspaper space.

Nell Kimball had nothing good to say of either of them.

BOOK FOUR

THE GIRLS

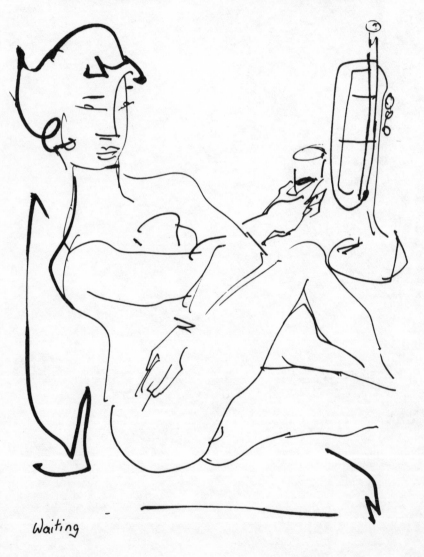

Waiting

Chapter 10

Enter Jazzing

Meanwhile, in the '80s the Negro was perfecting his music. Sporting house music-makers were eating. They were playing the popular and fancy music of the time, the sad ballads and the show music, the native songs from north and west, and the local tuner. But some of what they played and created was from their own lives, their church past, various versions of "Swing Low, Sweet Chariot." The church music had feeling. The laments in "On That Great Gittin'-Up Mornin'" and "I Hope My Mother Will Be There" reached a high level of folk art.

The Negro sang as he cut cotton or hoed 'taters, carried water, chopped cane, tied leaf-tobacco. He sang on the levee and on the railroad, shouted, hollered in the streets selling soft-shell crabs and York cabbage. He made it a street dance and a cakewalk, jig and ragtime stomps and struts; even kids sang hiding songs, ring songs, and street-corner rhymes. One ballad of sad fates and hard blows became "John Henry," who loved like a stallion and worked like a steamboat engine. There were gambling songs, songs of women, whores, yellow girls, songs of loving, fighting, razor brawls in dives and honky-tonks. Smoke and whiskey and tumbled desire all came into the music—low-down and mean, often beautiful and earnest toward God. It was everything inside the black man that was meat, work, love, and trouble. From "Lonely Woman Blues," to "I'm Goin' to Lift My Standard for My King," the music was satisfying—from children's voices respecting the Christ child, to the dirty-tone trombone notes about a man, a good man, and a bad woman in a bed.

It was still called whorehouse music, but the blues and the beat were popular in the street and in the dives—and at camp meetings and burial parties and housewarmings, in a life away from the sporting houses, away from Basin Street. The church colored folk lived free of vice and even married and went to pray. There was talk of educating the bright young ones, and Howard and Fiske and other schools produced musicians who could read notes. But they mostly went bad with concerts of Bach and Wagner and Victor Herbert. It was left to the lowly music-maker to carry the first strains of jazz forward all by himself.

Later, much later, when the whites heard it and played as much as they could their way, it was called Dixieland—not from the northern minstrel song, but most likely from the ten-dollar bill a local bank put out. On one side was printed the

Roadhouse Era

French word for ten, DIX. Ten dollars was an impressive sum and a person remembered it if he got a good ole "dix," real southern currency. Dixie in music came from Dix and later Dixie was used in general to mean the South. But at first Dixie and Dixieland meant *only* New Orleans. Then white men, such as Jack Laine, began to play jazz. They called his music Dixieland.

Jack Laine was born in 1873, and when he saw an alto horn he began to play. He played the drums too, but the alto horn was his real love. He played with the ragtime bands, with white groups that worked the picnics in Algiers across the bend of the Mississippi, at Kramer's Picnic Grounds, Milneburg on the lake, the racetrack, at fights, and wherever else music was needed. There were many Negro bands, but it wasn't until Jack Laine had his Ragtime Band that Dixieland was something good and important. The band had a clarinet, a cornet, alto horn, drums and key-trombone. For dancing there was added guitar, string-bass and violin, but no piano. That came later.

Laine had such men as Achille Baquet, clarinet; Lawrence Vega, cornet; Willy Guitar, string-bass; Dave Perkins, trombone, and Morton Abraham, guitar. They did 'Shadow Rag" and other rags. It was an "all-white band," even if two light-skinned Negros with blue eyes, Baquet and Perkins, were passing as whites. They did "Tiger Rag" under a new title, "Praline," and "Livery Stable Blues" as "Meatball." They ragged a tune by syncopating. They wore uniforms and rented themselves out for picnics, dance halls, and for advertising Ruskin Cigars.

One Negro, Dave Perkins passed for years. He had once played with Buddy Bolden. A white girl fell in love with him for a hectic affair. There was no solution and when it ended, the jazz man did the expected thing—he took to drink. He was sick and a colored girl nursed him back to life. Dave married her. The white music local withdrew his union card, because he was officially a Negro again.

Laine had a good clarinet player in Monty Korn, and in time Dixieland music was being played by other white bands— Johnny Fischer, Nunez, Massarini, and Bill Gallaty. The music was improvisation with hard and fast syncopation. Larry Shields did the best of the improvisations; he was very good on the clarinet. He had sock-making phrases in bursts with Leon LaRocco's early cornet on the melody. They had vibrant tones when they did "Lazy Daddy" or "High Society." Their ragtime may now seem thick with corn, but this was the beginning of white jazz. J. Russell Robinson could write down music and he worked out "Margie" and "Singing the Blues." Someone once described Dixieland as a revolution in 4-4 time.

Stale Bread Lacoume did a lot for jazz. He had a kid's street group called a spasm band. He played zither; the Cajun Willie Bussey, harmonica; Whisky Emile Benrod, home-made bass; Warm Gravy Cleve Craven, cheese-box banjo; Slew-Foot Pete Albert Montluzen, cigarbox-guitar. They worked for Doc Malney's Minstrel Show, but also in the sporting houses.

Stale Bread went blind. He added Dude Jimmy Lacoume, banjo; Sweet Potato Harry Carey, tambourine and cornet. They played riverboats and worked Toro's Basin Street. Later Stale Bread was at Halfway House with Rappolo and Brunies.

Music served as background in houses with rooms with mirrored walls and ceilings for circuses, indecent dancing, erotic displays. The brothels employed orchestras of from two to four, playing from seven o'clock to closing time at dawn.

There were other groups of musicians who played in the streets and saloons for coins and drinks. Some boys from twelve to fifteen years old called themselves The Spasm Band. These Spasm Boys had what might be termed the original jazz band. The manager and principal organizer, Harry Gregson, sang popular songs through a piece of gas pipe; he couldn't afford a megaphone. The boys screamed "hi-de-hi" and "ho-de-ho," expressions used in river songs.

The Spasm Band appeared in New Orleans in 1895, playing in front of theaters and in saloons and brothels; it also had a few engagements at the West End Grand Opera House. They serenaded Sarah Bernhardt. The Haymarket Dance Hall on Customhouse Street engaged experienced musicians as the Razy Dazy Spasm Band. The original Spasm Band made violent protest with stones and bricks, and the placards were changed to "Razy Dazy *Jazzy* Band!"

> *Rich gal she lives in a big brick house,*
> *Poor gal she lives in a frame.*
> *My gal she lives in the big new jail—*
> *But it's a brick house just the same.*

White women of certain warped emotional drives had been attracted to Negro men, and the black jazz men had even a stronger draw for the unhappy white woman. She saw in him

Beat Me Daddy

Livery Stable Blues

an image of forbidden passion, of animal drive. The pairing-off of white and black caused a loud noise of protest in the town. There was a lot of talk and a warning by the police to break this kind of thing up. On the surface the proper image of the pure southern woman was to remain like a banner of a partly lost war—at least until William Faulkner tore it to shreds in his novel *Sanctuary*, in which the white society girl, Temple Drake, is raped with a corncob in the hand of the impotent gangster Popeye, and put to work by him in a whorehouse. Her enjoyment of the process was a shocker, and it badly tattered the image of the southern girl.

There was a streak of sado-masochism in these women, as certain sociological studies show. Women bored by their protecting legend, aware of their husband's desires for brothel and Negro women, were driven to their own adventures. Tennessee Williams was to capture some of it in the character of Blanche in *Streetcar Named Desire*, who gives herself to a brute in New Orleans. Other writers of the South have given us the whole, or nearly all, of Krafft-Ebing's *Psychopathia Sexualis* as popular fiction, from *Tobacco Road* to the newest best sellers. Lesbianism, whips, pederasty, dead bodies in bed (Faulkner's *A Rose For Emily*), way-out ecstasies, fill the fiction of modern southern authors. Faulkner again and again draws a sordid picture of flagellation, adolescent promiscuity, and, in *Light in August*, a Negro man, white woman love.

Dissolute themes, diabolic matings, idiot offspring of strange psychological guilts stain the modern literature of the southland. Truman Capote and Tennessee Williams bring in homosexual decadence on southern streets, on old plantations, the leering limp-wristed invitation hiding under fine old manners in decaying houses. Anything that happened in the sporting houses since the French first came became themes for writers.

Conventional morality was badly wrinkled, and the underworld of New Orleans showed in just what ways a society could break down sexually.

> *Let her go, let her go, God bless her*
> *Wherever she may be,*
> *She may roam the whole world over*
> *She'll never find a sweet man like me.*

On Dauphine and Burgundy Street white women and Negresses were patronized by men of all colors. The press reported:

> *In our daily walks through life we notice the surprising amount of co-habitation of white men with Negro women. And this thing of white girls becoming enamored of Negroes is becoming rather too common. In Dauphine and Burgundy Streets, Canal to Toulouse Streets nearly every building is a brothel. Streets swarm with streetwalkers and fancy men. Some put a piece of carpet on the sidewalk and entertain customers in view of passersby. Pails of hot water were kept to discourage use of the doorsteps. Inside prices were fifteen to fifty cents; on the sidewalk a dime. Many women were addicted to the whip and were served by a specialist, who at his trade of flagellant was called Joe the Whipper. He carried a black bag for the tools of his trade—switches, whips, flexible metal rods, cat of nine-tails. [He worked for years unmolested, servicing his clients powerfully.]*

The musicians were not paid as well as Joe the Whipper, but they made a living. Those who could attract a white mistress had the added danger of being waylaid if she came from a good family, and being murdered, or, at the least, castrated. Yet so strong was the drive that the pairing of white and black in no way abated.

The women who worked in the sporting houses were hardly better off. Agents, recruiters, procuresses, were an active part of the local business scene. Surplus whores were also exported to Memphis, Atlanta, and other southern redlight districts. A girl from a fashionable New Orleans house came as if from a good finishing school: "the new girl in town."

Not all solid citizens dared go to sporting houses. There were discreet little flats, assignation houses where very young girls would wait for clients who wanted something not yet ripe, and on the quiet.

Stock, as the younger girls were called, *fresh stock* if under fifteen, were available to clients who were listed in the books of the proper madames. Youth came high and a school teacher and procuress named Louisa Murphy sold these school-days, golden-rule-days Lolitas for eight hundred dollars a child.

Waiting lists often took a year to fill. Virgins commanded a steady market price of two hundred to four hundred dollars each. One girl at first was willing, then broke away on the way to an assignation and sued the employment agency for "injury to my character." The court gave her fifty dollars' damages for that and the agent was warned not to attract attention in this manner again. By 1890 the maidenhead market was glutted, and virgins could be bought for fifty dollars. The horror is that there was no horror—no one seemed to care for long.

One agent expressed her problems to a reporter:

> *I frequently receive orders from the keepers of fashionable places. These ladies ask me to send them girls, or women for that matter. I always prefer to have experienced women than virtuous girls, because there is less fear of trouble. I am in correspondnce with women like Molly Wates and Abbie Allen of Galveston; these people write to me for girls. Some time ago I received an order from Miss Abbie Allen to send her some girls and soon after Miss Lena Smith informed me that she could secure two nice young girls. I do not like to have anything to do with innocent girls. . . . Not a very long time ago a mother brought her three daughters to me and offered them for sale. . . . Two, she said, were bad, and the youngest still unacquainted with vice and the wickedness of the world. She demanded $25 for the girls and expressed her belief that she ought to get more for the guileless maiden. I bought the girls and made a nice profit.*

This lust for virgins is hard to explain. It was a messy business. It led to dangers from revengeful fathers and brothers, and there were always the many hard laws of society to punish those who sought for what was called *cherry, quail,* and later *nymphets.* Some explain it as male vanity, a desire to be the first among the innocent, the unpoluted, the wrapped package, the pioneer invader of new territory. But vanity does not explain it all. Sadism is part of it, the tainted sinner assaulting untouched virtue. Cruelty, or just the power to be cruel, is more the modern pattern; in this way, perhaps, all womanhood is punished through one frail object; a man may revenge himself on Mom, debauch the tradition of sacred womanhood,

Room Service

Morning

even go against the dogma and theology of holy virginity. All these reasons have been given and are depicted, for example, in the plays of Tennessee Williams and others.

> *There was a young maiden*
> *Who played a guitar,*
> *Played a guitar.*
> *He told her he loved her,*
> *But oh, how he lied.*

There was also a fancy market, not small by any means, for male degenerates. Homosexuality was a hidden thing in the South but it was then as powerful a force, under the rug of society, as now. A public scandal such as the trial of Oscar Wilde did a little to bring the practice into the public view. The perverts were hard driven to find partners. While buggery was the farm boy's joke and was prevalent along with incest in the bypaths of the tobacco roads, middle and upper class homosexuality had to hide in dark corners, as in Proust's world, and place its destiny in the paws of greedy people.

On Baronne Street a Miss Carol could always find boys for the trade. Young Negro boys of light color were in demand. They were known as "goldskins" and were often pampered and spoiled by white protectors. Most of the boys were hungry youngsters, often without homes or parents. Some were vicious blackmailers, and the white faggot often got more than he contracted for. Miss Carol was the secret partner in a homosexual establishment, the madame there being a man called

Miss Big Nellie. The inmates, all men, in drag or out, were called Lady Richard, Lady Fresh, Chicago Belle, Toto and a few titles hardly fit to print.

For homosexuals the special season of balls and fetes were gala times at Big Nellie's house. The shrill cry of voices and laughter filled the house during the fitting of costumes, designing and dressmaking; rubber female anatomies and wig curling were all the rage. There was no color line and the guests, Negroes and whites, mixed at these balls making their play for the gloriously gowned inmates.

Nell Kimball says of Miss Big Nellie's:

> *I never had much to do with that kind of Greek stuff, and I lost some clients who raved about the balls and costumes of the drag joints. I always figured there was something wrong with a John if he had to get his kicks watching fake women carry on and cop each other's joints. The only time I ever was inside Big Nellie's was the night an old customer came to me and said his son, who was down from Yale, was going there with a freakish friend and he feared trouble. He didn't dare go himself to get the boy home. Would I?*
>
> *I got Harry and went over to Baronne Street, and Harry got us through the back door. It was a hell of a queen's ball at two in the morning. Most of the gowns were off, and some of the most respectable people you ever saw were playing at soixante-neuf on the staircase, and a daisy chain was going full blast in the parlor. Someone grabbed me but he found the tit was real; he didn't stay. Harry got hold of the kid, real drunk and rouge smeared on his face, but we had no trouble getting him out and home in a carriage. Big Nellie said he didn't mind. "The chicken was so scared he was no use at all and was just a wet blanket on the party."*

I was always against the fairies because they gave the district a bad name, and I always figured God didn't mean a man to turn away from a woman and go at it nasty with another man. Some of the lavendar group used to come to my house; those were the bi-sexual ones. Later the joke was they were AC and DC like the electric currents. The girls didn't like faggots either. Sometimes a John wanted a boy and girl together for this pleasuring, but I didn't cater to such tastes. I ran a good old-fashioned whorehouse and they knew what I had to offer, and if they didn't like it, they could go elsewhere. I'll say this, there were plenty of places in New Orleans they could get what they wanted.

The police and the people higher up didn't like trouble either. The cribs and the sidewalk workers were run out from Burgundy to Conti Street, and the parlor houses were permitted to take care of the trade in a better atmosphere. Of course costs went up all the time and taxes were pushed higher. Some of the houses had trouble. But I ran a good tight house and didn't toss money around where it didn't show, so I never had big trouble in that direction. I also had backers in high places who held about fifty percent of the shares in the house.

Nell doesn't go into detail as to just who her backers were except to say they were highly respectable and that some ran the city, some made state laws, some were merchants.

The houses that got into trouble didn't meet their bills and ran into debt. The W. B. Ringrose Furniture Emporium sued Carrie Freeman, Mary O'Brien, Mattie Marshall, Nellie Williams, and Sally Levy, brothel-keepers, for $7,000 for furniture bought on credit. Mattie owed the Ringrose store $5,000 and Carrie owed them $1,300. The madames were fortunate in tax assessments. Many were not assessed at all, including Fanny

Decker, Frankie Belmont, and Annie Merritt. Annie conducted business in person until eighty years old. She smoked a dozen cigars a night.

> *Wish I was an apple,*
> *Hangin' from a tree.*
> *Baby, pluck me off,*
> *Take a bite of me.*

Chapter 11

The Real Storyville

Like the Tenderloin of New York, the Barbary Coast of San Francisco or even Sodom and Gomorrah, Storyville took on legendary qualities that were only slightly related to truth. Actually Storyville's true story is often more fascinating and dramatic than the myth, the dream, the sensational projection of its indecencies and sexual fantasies.

Storyville was created because harlotry, crime, and the importing of whores and their sweet daddies, fancy men and protectors, were getting out of hand in New Orleans. By the middle of the 1880's the queen of the sporting houses was Gertie Livingston in the old Peed House on Burgundy Street, run, as she put it, for "a nice class of trade." Her girls were feisty and given to the use of fingernails and fists and any weapon at hand including the *boite a l'ordure*. One of her girls bit off another girl's finger in a fight and was tossed out into the street, the madame holding her trunk because it contained four dozen towels. As one paper put it: "Helen does not think Gertie has any right to withhold the trunk, as the towels come under the act that provides that a workman's tools cannot be retained."

Date

The perverse pride of Gertie Livingston's sporting house was a girl known as Josephine Icebox. In a district where wild passion was faked and a girl was taught to act out the orgasm in the manner of a method actress, Josephine Icebox was the attraction for those men who felt she was a challenge to their sex. The studs of the town saw in her frigidity a sort of icy holy grail. Some said a prize of ten dollars (in house pleasures) was offered to anyone who could get her emotionally involved in the act of copulation. There is no record of any winners, at least no names have come down in sporting house history.

Leader of the new reform party that was finally to produce a legal redlight district under city control was the Reverend E. A. Clay, who had been at work saving nymphets from the whorehouses. In 1892 he began to preach sermons about the evil of the sporting houses that were spreading all over town.

Laws requiring medical examinations as compulsory for "all women and girls notoriously abandoned to lewdness" had failed because the respectable women of the city had gathered to protest loudly against "this nasty *insult* to Southern women!" The pudenda, commercial or not, was sacred and not for medical inspection, even if several important families produced idiot and deformed children caused by infections resulting from their father's visiting down the line. A law to inspect harlots was fought by other pious groups on the grounds that "the law would recognize the existence of whores and whorehouses."

The idea to make the whore legal was not new, as a news item shows:

Organize a trade union for prostitutes? The idea seemed stunning in 1907, when trade-unionism was new and the oldest profession still flourishing. Actress Florence Farr got to wondering what sort of person would be best suited to run such an organization, and she put the question to just the right man: Playwright George Bernard Shaw, who himself had exhibited a fatherly concern for the girls in Mrs. Warren's Profession. *Well, mused Shaw in his reply, "the project seems pretty utopian." For one thing, he wrote, the people engaged in the trade "are the loudest detractors of it," while its "protectors" are "of extraordinarily good character." But perhaps the union job "could be done by a very energetic, muscular and violent woman, with the devotion of a saint and the arbitrariness and executive power of a prizefighter." No one fitting that description appeared on the scene, and the idea of an International Sisterhood of Doxies died.*

In January of 1897, Alderman Sidney Story made history. He was a stockbroker, involved mostly in cotton futures, rice, and tobacco, who claimed to have made a deep and detailed study of prostitution and its regulations "in the capitols of Europe." There were those who hinted he had merely been a customer on his travels abroad. But he seems to have been a sincere man and a good citizen.

He proposed a city ruling to permit the setting aside of certain sections of the French Quarter of the city of New Orleans where prostitution would be able to do its business. It was not, as most historians state, to be legalized. Permitted, but *not* made so by law. It was one of the blindfold games that Americans have often played with vice, winking at it, trying to control it, while saying it isn't really there.

Band Singer.

Of course there was debate. The police and the political grafters had to be reassured there would still be an income from regulating and seeing that certain rules were enforced. By July of 1897 the Story ordinance was remolded to provide for *two* segregated districts, one in the French Quarter and the other above Canal Street. So it came to pass.

> BE IT ORDAINED, *by the Common Council of the City of New Orleans, That Section I, of Ordinance 13,032 C.S., be and the same is hereby amended as follows: From and after the first of October, 1897, it shall be unlawful for any prostitute or woman notoriously abandoned to lewdness, to occupy, inhabit, live or sleep in any house, room or closet, situated without the following limits, viz: From the South side of Customhouse Street to the North side of St. Louis Street, and from the lower or wood side of North Basin Street to the lower or wood side of Robertson Street: 2nd:—And from the upper side of Perdido Street to the lower side of Gravier Street, and from the river side of Franklin Street to the lower or wood side of Locust Street, provided that nothing herein shall be so construed as to authorize any lewd woman to occupy a house, room or closet in any portion of the city. It shall be unlawful to open, operate or carry on any cabaret, concert-saloon or place where can can, clodoche or similar female dancing or sensational performances are shown, without the following limits, viz: from the lower side of N. Basin Street to the lower side of N. Robertson Street, and from the south side of Customhouse Street to the north side of St. Louis Street.*

To control things — and, one suspects, to continue the graft — there were fines from five to twenty-five dollars and imprisonment up to thirty days in default of payment, for violations of the ordinance; the Mayor to close any house, within or without the segregated district, that "may become dangerous to public morals" and require the occupants to move. If not, the Mayor could place a policeman at the door to warn away all parties who undertook to enter.

The days of Liberty Hall were here. At the end of the nineteenth century the oldest profession was still not being ruined by amateurs. New Orleans was proud, and ashamed, of its cathouses. Citizens bragged about them and the girls, advertised them, shook hands, and counted up the profits.

The jazz man could have gotten along without the madames and their parlors, and he didn't have to be a part of the sinful living. But it happened that way. He had music, they had the need. He wasn't any more sinful or lustful; he seemed so because he was there. He didn't waste it. He was there to play ragtime, the blues, and jazz. That was his job. The rest was gravy. Maybe girls loved him best — and some jazz men doubled in stud. But it was all business in the grind-mills. The big money went to the respectable bankers and churches who owned the land, the houses with the mirrored rooms and the beds with red plush hangings. Whorehouses were a poor folk's trade and a rich man's pleasure.

Storyville democratically tried to serve all price ranges, but it was a place where money counted. The jazz man, like all the rest of the house, the girls and the madame, lived a lot on tips. A riled-up sensualist and a spender, crying over "My Ol' Kentucky home," or "She Was Only a Bird in a Gilded Cage," could drop a five dollar goldpiece into a kitty, a vase set on top of the piano. Even the girls liked to ask for a bottle of perfume

Hostess.

Stephen Longstreet

for an extra effort, and the perfume sold by the house was as phony as their passionate tossing.

With a public right to be in business the houses could hire house bands and the music could be louder. Vice was now acceptable.

> *Seems like money, seems I'm dead,*
> *But I'm satisfied,*
> *Yes, I'm satisfied.*

In the French Quarter — bounded by Customhouse and St. Louis Street and North Basin and Robertson — the district was named ironically by the inmates and their sports for the Alderman Story, and became the famous Storyville, forty lively blocks of vice, music, drink, and laughter.

For two decades the tenderloin along Basin Street was to sport jazz. Storyville became and stayed the biggest vice attraction in the nation. Tom Anderson, its unofficial mayor, had his city hall in the Arlington Annex Saloon. He printed and sold *The Blue Book* at a quarter a shot, the full directory and guide of the sporting houses, listing the names of the working girls and the entertainers to be found in the houses. Every place had a piano player and often a band and trio. Singers and dancers entertained the girls and guests. The first pianist on record in Storyville was for Countess Piazza's *maison de joie*. He claimed he was John the Baptist. Then Tony Jackson took over and his big hit was "I've Got Elgin Movements in My Hips with Twenty Years' Guarantee." One of the first blues singers in Storyville, Anne Cook, was featured at the redlighted number of Countess Willie Piazza, the pacesetter of the district.

Basin Street had the Mahogany Hall run by Lulu White, known as the Diamond Queen. She had diamonds every place but in her nose. She had a mirrored room and the most beautiful octoroons, known as far west as Frisco. Lulu kept a good piano and Al Carrel, Clarence Williams, and Richard Jones worked for her at various times. Williams did the place proud with "Mahogany Hall Stomp."

A thirteen-year-old kid came in from Gulfport and went to work for Tom Anderson's Annex. In Storyville he was soon called Jelly Roll Morton. He hit a good piano and worked out the "King Porter Stomp."

A few years ago a survivor of the coming of jazz to New Orleans gave an interview in which he recalled those wild days. George Lewis, an old clarinetist was one of the Negro pioneers playing "All the Girls Like the Way I Ride." His life is typical of most of the jazz men of the time:

> Lewis' mother wanted him to be a violinist. When he was seven, she gave him a quarter to buy a toy violin. The store was out of toy violins and he bought a fife. He was 16 when he got his first clarinet for $4. He was a year older when the family moved to Mandeville near New Orleans and he became a member of the Black Eagle Band. Then he played with Buddy Petit's Black and Tan Band and finally returned to New Orleans. Lewis followed the street and marching bands in what was called the "second line," and, like most, wound up playing in the tonks of Storyville.
> In his time Lewis played at least 500 funerals, the same number of street parades and uncounted weddings, chris-

Blues Singer

Saturday Night

tenings and picnics, the latter for the most part on the shores of Lake Pontchartrain, at places called West End, Spanish Fort and Milneburg. The first and the third have been celebrated in song: "West End Blues" and "Milneburg Joys." The latest funeral played by Lewis was that of Oscar (Papa) Celestin, the fine old trumpeter.

About Celestin's funeral Lewis commented, "I didn't feel very good about it, but we wanted to give him a nice send-off. He was a wonderful man. They buried him in the Mount Olive Cemetery. They had two bands, the Eureka, which was my band, and the Tuxedo. We didn't play on the way back from the cemetery. It was cold that day. But the bands were his wishes. And they are mine. I always told my people when I pass, that's what I'd like. I've played funerals for corner bums. I played some I didn't get anything at all for. And I always said, I want the music, too. That's the way a musician feels. The music is something hard to explain. Anything we would play would be jazz. In the old days we lived more like a family. Now everybody's strangers to each other, mostly. Then there were fifteen or twenty good bands."

He married at 19, fathered eleven children, of whom five are alive, and never left New Orleans until he came up North with the band organized by the late Willie (Bunk) Johnson. He has a six-room home in Algiers across the river from New Orleans, and thinks he has got about as much out of life as he wants.

"I make a better living for my family and myself. We eat better. I got a lot of burdens taken out of my mind. We don't have the worriments where we're going to make it or how to pay the rent. It was real hard, I can tell you. The houses weren't sufficient to live in then. Rats and roaches running around. I remember a house we lived in at Saint Claude at Ursaline. We had to take a stick to the rats, we were that afraid they'd bite the children. I got nothing to complain about."

Storyville was a busy place after dark — the big mansions thick with music early in the evening before things got going.

217

The naked girls in the cheap cribs, the lavish brothels looking down on four-bit trade, and every place the players of jazz at work. They played in parades and at church burials by day, and in Storyville joints at night. Dives, saloons, and houses of assignation grew to see the new music as their own, and they liked it because it was sensual; no shame or furtiveness, no sinful grimace. Jazz gave the rhythm to Storyville, and Storyville brought to jazz vice, drink, and later, marijuana. Life was fast, crude, evil, and the jazz was a slice of society hard to sweep under the rug.

> Oh tell me how long
> Must I wait?
> Can't I get it now
> Or must I hesitate?

The houses inspired songs, some blue, and singers to tour and sing them. There was Ma Rainey, and later Bessie Smith. Ma and Bessie sang it the way they felt. Jelly Roll Morton transformed them in his own way. He gave them lyric polish, almost French elegance. He added, from ragtime, and he pushed out the horizon of harmonic and melodic ideas. Not an easy man to get along with, he knew he was good and that his bump of ego was touched with genius. A creative jazz man, a performer, part naive, part mean, Jelly Roll lived inside himself, getting lyric, distilling his love of the jazz form. His accompaniment was the merging of voice and piano doing a great job: "Winnin' Boy," "I Thouht I Heard Buddy Bolden Say," "Doctor Jazz," and "Michigan Water Blues."

My Sister Kate.

In contrast there was Hociel Thomas, the powerhouse of the early blues singers. But not for sinful music. She stuck to the churchlike blues. It was a hard world for the colored woman, churchly *or* sinful.

> *I'm tellin' you, lover,*
> *How you strut that thing*
> *Night and day.*
>
> *Gettin' sick and tired of the way you do,*
> *God, Mama gonna pizon you.*
>
> *Sprinkle goofer dust on your bed,*
> *Wake up some mornin'*
> *Find yourself dead . . .*

It looked like Storyville would always be there. But would it?

Americans can't accept vice as part of the full sad human picture. They listen with their inner ear to the voices of a Puritan past. To soften their guilt they make vice glamorous, dress it up and pose it in melodrama, create legends and songs about it. Music was often considered the best part of vice. Even the church organ was suspect in many groups. Beyond the voices raised in sacred hymns music could be the devil's playmate. The Maypole of New England was often burned and its dancers jailed. Music on the frontier and at hell-fire camp meetings could lead to hasty and sudden matings in pine-clearings. The actress and the singers were considered prostitutes and pimps with a sideline.

Hustling Storyville took on that legendary shine of sin that is always part of the American dream, from the Tenderloin district to the Barbary Coast. Trapped in this native sense of sin was jazz. Storyville without jazz would have existed but it wouldn't have sounded the same.

Storyville was Sight Number One in those days, and the visitor came out of the Southern Railroad Station on Canal Street looking for a hack or the early taxis. He'd head for a hotel, and then for a night on the town. White or black. And the Yankee tried the wild colored joints first of all.

> Gimme a pigfoot
> An' a bottle of beer.
> Send me gate I don't care.
> Gimme a reefer
> An' a gang of gin,
> Slay me cause
> I'm in my sin.

Jazz every night. It was a hard life for the jazz man but the only one he wanted. You started at eight at night and played until the last customer left silently. A buck a night, sometimes two or two-fifty, and tips when they let you pass the hat. It was all going to last forever, or longer. There would be chicken and Brunswick stew and corn-pone and pot likker and gumbo for all. Fancy clothes, diamond rings, and everything.

> Cause I'm crazy about my lovin',
> Must have it all the time,
> It takes a brownskin woman
> To satisfy my mind . . .

221

BOOK FIVE

LIBERTY HALL

Big Time for Jazz

Chapter 12

Riding the Beat

The first great jazz man to come out of Storyville was Joseph (King) Oliver, born in 1885. He grew up on Dryades Street and his family set down at Nashville and Coliseum Avenues. It was a big time for jazz. Buddy Bolden was fancy man and Bunk Johnson was setting cornet style. Joe Oliver played in a child's brass band, slow to learn music, the written stuff, the old way of putting it down and playing proper. When he was fifteen he went with the boys' brass band on tour by steamboat to Baton Rouge. It was a tough time for touring Negroes. Joe got a knife scar over one eye. Too big for kid bands, and other jobs hard to get, he became a butler for a white family.

Joe played his horn in the servants' rooms, he played with bands, and the white folk let him train a boy in his place when he had to play. He tried for the Eagle Band but they said he was loud, bad. Joe Oliver had been impressed by written-down music and soon he got the knack of it. He buttled and played at Negro funerals and worked out a variation on the old hymn, "Sing On," that nobody wanted to miss. Joe worked hard, listened to Bunk Johnson and soon sent out a stomp of his own, "Dippermouth." That was his trademark. Everybody used to shout out for "Dippermouth."

Joe joined Manuel Perez' Onward Brass Band, and in no time he was playing in Storyville, his horn wide open like the place. He played with the Aberdeen Brothers in a place at the corner of Bienville and Marais with Big Eye Louis, Deedee Chandler and Dick Jones. Joe began to blow in B-flat. One night he walked out into the street blowing. The street stopped to listen. No one had ever done it like that.

He was King Oliver. He led his own band at Lala's Cafe with Lorenzo Tio, Zue Robinson, Buddy Christian, and Zino. Lala's became the place to hear the best. Jazz lovers, tourists, the sporting men all came to Lala's to hear King Oliver blow his horn. When the night was over for the customers, the Storyville players would come to Lala's and put on a session of their own, Joe blowing, the music getting different, everyone taking turns in trying out his solos. So jazz grew a little more in the streets, the river and the marsh mists at morning finding tired jazz men going home to get some sleep.

When they closed Storyville, there were a lot of men who

Clarinets

couldn't get work. Even King Oliver found tough times. So he went north and the first public playing he did in Chicago was under the El trains in the Loop playing tail-gate trombone with a wagon to get people to buy Liberty Bonds. He blew New Orleans jass (not jazz) on Wabash Street. He played at two South Side joints. The Creole Jass Band at the *Royal Garden Blues* set his style.

New Orleans was lost, but King Oliver didn't change much. He remained a horn player from the south, eating a plate of hominy, half-a-dozen hamburgers, a quart of milk for lunch. Besides food, King liked pool, baseball and jazz.. They missed his horn on the delta.

The piano in the French Quarter was always a sign of class. No sporting house lacked one. It came late to jazz but made for itself a place and a way of playing; ragtime, barrelhouse, later boogie-woogie. But the piano player played mostly because there was a living in it—a chance for a drink, to play for friends, to let a new idea in his brain out through the ends of his fingers.

The Negro at a jazz piano disregarded its limitations. He never heard of them. Up to 1900 there had been a few barrel-house players among the kegs of whiskey. All they left were their names: Old Florida Sam, Bricky Johnny, Trigger Sam, Skinny-Head Pete. The ragtime boys had class. Al Carroll, Al Wilson, Sam Davis played it as whorehouse music. Jelly Roll and Tony Jackson could even sing it. Blue piano, hot piano, jazz piano. The sporting houses had them.

Clarinet Master

Fight in a Jazz Joint

The first piano players drifted around playing guitar when there was no piano, hit it solid transposing the chord and the rhythm, patterning the way they felt it in their heads. Barrelhouse was primitive and archaic, but real. It touched ragtime It was stomp and it was blue. But it didn't make it on a teak or rosewood concert grand.

Jelly Roll once explained how he got the ideal jazz piano:

Find a saloon or a madame that owns a battered upright. Old and loose in action. If it's in tune, beat it until it takes on that special out-of-tune twang. The bright boys they call that jazz dissonance on the blue scale. Pick a crate with a mandolin attachment so that when the plucked note is right you got yourself almost a harpsichord, and don't make your sound too clean. The old dirty tone is barrelhouse blues. To get that pad the piano strings with old newspapers or some burlap bag and kick the front board hard for drum rhythm. Don't care how it looks, just attention how it sounds. They don't make pianos like that no more.

Barrelhouse on concert grands? No. Rumshop piano is the only kind to grind out "Barrelhouse Woman," "Shreveport Farewell," and the "Harry Brown Blues." Keep that treble tremoloandi on the ground bass, and end in the descending bass. The slow blues, a walking bass going up, coming down, and the beat of a breathing locomotive. Yeah!

In Storyville the music went from ragtime to jazz in a generation. Ragtime had a fine metrical accent, but that wasn't the true jazz. Ragtime went towards jazz with a continuously suspended rhythm in the right direction.

Ragtime first appeared in 1896 as the word "Ragtime" on music used by Bert Williams, the Negro comic in his song,

"Oh, I Don't Know, You're Not So Warm." Ragtime was fluidity and rhythmic suspensions and was written down.

Negro music fit the personal needs, explained the brooding ideas of trouble, of women. A way of living that didn't expect the beautiful or the perfect.

Before the horn and the piano came, fiddlers and banjo players did it for jigs, reels, cotillions and contra-danses. The mandolin, guitar and string-bass and the pebble-filled gourd helped. Cutting contests caught on—tests in improvisation. The early jazz man couldn't read music; those that did were rare. Some said, "I can read music-notes but I can't separate 'em."

Jazz was a lot of things and had many names: jabo, jaba, jazpation, jazynco, jazorient, jazanola. Also, jazanata, jazarella, jazanjaz. Even jazology, jazette, jazitis and jazioso.

Popular sporting house songs were arranged as jazz and the music was good if played right. The trumpet invented middle register solos and soon blues singers tried it—Mammie Smith, Clara Smith, Butterbeans and Susie, Maggie Jones, Lilli Delk Christian and Bessie Smith.

Louis Armstrong, born at the turn of the century, had been a kid running around town singing tenor with a Perdido Street quartette. Storyville knew Louis and Happy, Shots and Kid Rena. Louis, a tenor, dreaming of singing bass, playing a four-string guitar with a flat-wood neck, a cigarbox body. He hung out where Buddy Bolden's band warmed up. He learned to whistle with the players.

Blue Guitar

Armstrong spent his time away from the Waif's Home on a Vieux Carré cart peddling coal.

> *My mule is white,*
> *My face is black!*
> *I sell my coal*
> *Two bits a sack!*

It was the place for free band instruments and Louis got a cornet from Joseph Jones, Captain of the Home. Louis learned to blow the way he liked it. He cut notches in the cornet mouthbit to keep it firm against his lip. He blew and his lip became tough. Peter Davis at the Home taught him to read some. He came out of the Home a good horn-player, too young for a band job. He shot crap, peddled papers, ran errands for the madames. And there was coal—filling a gunny sack with coal dropped by loaders, always a way to make two bits, but never much more.

Louis grew. There was a girl named Daisy Parker. She liked to swing and mix it up. He and Daisy danced and sat by the Eagle Band stand and listened to Bunk Johnson play cornet. Louis got to playing spots in dives around Gravier Street, making a buck a night. Joe Oliver was coming along and Louis was studying his style. He organized a band in the Oliver manner with little Joe Lindsay.

Louis married Daisy. Things got bad at home and he went on the river with Fate Marable's Jazz-E-Saz Band. On the Strekfus line boats with the boating parties and fine men working with him—Pop Foster, Dave Jones, Baby Dodds, Picou,

The King

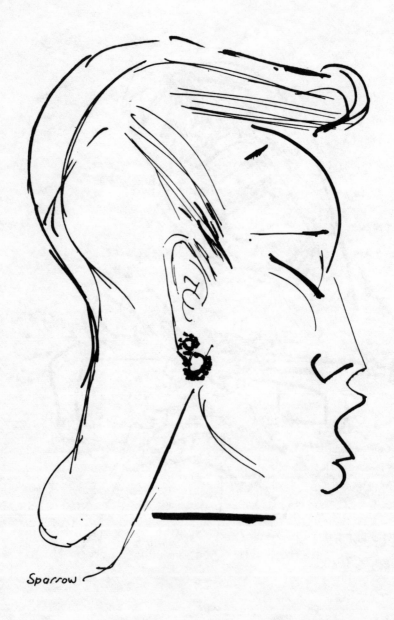

Sparrow

Sam Dutrey. After a season Louis settled on Burgundy Street with Zut Singleton's band at the Orchard Cabaret. Then over to Tommy Anderson's Real Thing on Rampart Street. Louis tried his hand at writing music. He got fifty dollars for his right to "I Wish That I Could Shimmy Like My Sister Kate." Louis Armstrong was growing into a great horn man.

One summer day after Storyville was closed there came a telegram from Joe Oliver in Chicago for Louis to get up there and play second cornet in the band. Louis packed his bag and fitted right in with a good horn. Joe enjoyed the twenty-two year old boy who was soon going to outplay him.

Lil Hardin, the piano player, took Louis under her care. Lil had education and had planned to play classical piano. But she made jazz history. She began by playing piano in a music store, for three dollars a week. She played first for Sugar John's New Orleans Jazz Band, then King Oliver got her. She fell for Louis. Daisy became the ex-Mrs. Armstrong; it all became proper and fitting and legal. And New Orleans and the joints lost Louis Armstrong for good.

But what of the white jazz men who played Dixieland?

Leon Joseph Rappolo took lessons on piano from Professor Carrie (a cathouse piano-player), switched to clarinet, stealing his old man's. Leon's father sent him to Santa Guriffe to learn reading and notes. Leon learned ragtime from Eddie Cherie, part Negro, passing. Leon ran away to play in a pit band with Bee Palmer on the Orpheum Circuit when he was fourteen. At seventeen he was playing with the New Orleans Rhythm Kings,

Alone

about to travel to Chicago to carry Dixieland. Leon, between the girls, booze and marijuana had a brilliant start but no future.

To be a jazz pioneer was a tough row, and it got to you. Sauce, reefers, or you froze to death too stewed to move; hacking cough, the shakes; a lot of things happened. It was grief to a lot of men who had respect for the jazz they took and made their own in their own way as they pushed the beat.

Is all this sound lost?

Recording the Rhythm Kings relaxed the Original Dixieland style a bit, and got it rhythmically closer to Negro beat. You can hear some of the original Dixieland Jazz Band recordings done in 1917. The Rhythm Kings started recording in 1921. The first big Negro recordings are King Oliver's Creole Jazz Band in 1922. Acoustically recorded, often by second-rate companies; it's all that's left. Sold as "Electrically Recorded," they often meant the electric light bulb that lit up the place. The clarity and balance is sometimes very good. But it's only a scratchy echo of the music the New Orleans sporting houses once gave the world.

Street Musicians

Oh I love to hear my baby
Call my name,
She can call it so easy
And so doggone plain . . .

Of the sporting houses at this time, Nell Kimball wrote:

You had to stay on your toes when Storyville was going
along with the law, for the graft went on just the same and
they could close you up for an ashcan left in the wrong
spot or for leaky plumbing, or keeping old newspapers
out back as a fire hazard. Any of a dozen little things
would be found to be against the regulations. I always
had good protection because of the people higher up who
had shares in the house. Still it was a problem getting the
right girls and keeping them in order, not letting their
fancy men over-run the place, keeping the likker from
being stolen.

Now that no one could raid a hook-shop or house for
indecency, lewdness or prostitution, the places could be
run with more attention to details. In the first years of the
century (and we had a real high jinks New Year welcom-
ing the new time) there was a kind of breakdown of the
conventional ways of doing things, you might say the
morality was getting loose and slipping. But it wasn't until
1914 that everything went haywire and you couldn't keep
up the standards anymore. Whip workers were in demand,
le vice anglais the sports in uniform began to call it. The
erotic shows had to be livlier and a bit crazy. The old times
were going and I knew it when coquetterie gave way to
dance crazes like the Castle Walk and the Bunny Hug, the
Johns almost dancing holes in the parlor rugs. They still
drank champagne, but the cocktail was popular and Harry
had to keep up with the latest kind of mixed drinks. The
whores were skinnier too. I still had a couple of featherbed
girls, really women, bulging with knobs and curves, so the
old clients were kept happy. But the slim girls were in
demand, Gibson, Anna Held, Kellerman types, and I had
to bring in girls I wouldn't have used as rat bait in the old
days when Lillian Russell was at her best. I didn't stay

around for the flapper days that followed the Great War, but I used to hear the madames that came to Florida for a rest complaining about the damn girls, looking like boys, that they had to fill in with.

One professor, not a piano player, I mean a real double-dome who often came to the house on Basin Street, he used to sit in his underwear in the back parlor and talk about the breakdown of this and the breakdown of that and give out with sociological stuff that I never got any head or tail of. He said the whole world was changing its habits. He was a nice old coot and was involved with what in the trade is called a gamahucker. I could feel the change of habits after 1914 in the way people went crazy and prices went up; and I raised the charge too, and cut down the time a bit, and frankly, now I was using colored girls; browns and yellows and golds and no longer calling them Spanish or Chinese. There was a breaking down of some of the old standards, but I still kept out of voodoo and the faggot and Lesbian acts and the blue movie stuff. Some of the houses were showing movies made in France, but I always prided myself we could do almost anything they could show with our own talent—if someone would pay the price.

I kept out the nuts who would abuse the girls, whippers, of course, were part of the show, and I had two hard butt girls who rather liked it, so it wasn't abuse but pleasure, I suppose.

The girls were getting cheeky, too, when it looked like we would be getting into the war. I was recruiting them where I could and I even had a real society woman, which I had always been against. She lived up near Lake Charles where she had a husband and children, but she liked rough handling, and they were very socially prominent and wealthy up at Lake Charles. Alice, that's what she called herself, she liked to come down for a week with us when we got a lot of real tough trade; ship riveters with big pay checks and new rich truckers; all kinds of mean and hard people who make it big in a war. They were never in a house as classy as mine before, and they really tore things

239

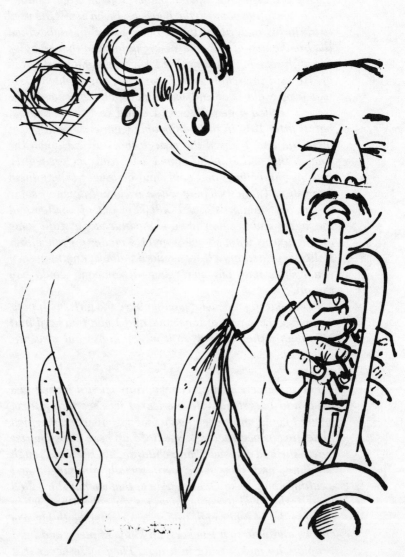

Strip Show

240

up but paid for them. Alice liked them, craved them, the rougher, the more unwashed the better. She never could be worked over enough and some of these lummoxes and shipworkers in their new silk shirts, and even spats, would really give her a rough time. She had ecstasies, she would tell me Monday noon, leaving for Lake Charles, battered, pale as a fish belly, hardly able to stand, but happy. It was this kind of thing — outsiders for kicks — that was really bringing down the sporting house trade, only we didn't see it at the time.

As I've said, wars always make sex a kind of disease and even send off a whole epidemic of rape and horniness. We felt it in Storyville in several ways when the war grew bigger and bigger. A lot of the Johns were finding outlets in their country clubs and in pickups, not street walkers on round heels but women they met at tea dances and in hotel lobbies out for an afternoon of sport, or to earn a little excitement and maybe a flask of perfume. Also we began to get the boys younger and younger in their tight army tunics and boots and the Sam Browne belts. Officers in training, and Navy Reserve officers. New Orleans was a big Naval yard and training station and at first it looked like the gold rush of '49 all over again for the sporting houses.

But something was wrong, and I talked with the other madames and they felt it too. I didn't read the newspapers much; the girls hardly touched them, their reading being novels and dream books and astrology, if they could read. They became slovenly and I had to have Harry take the leather to them a bit, or rough them up. But they'd leave by the fire escape or just not come back on their day off with their sweet daddy or some officer stud. Wars may be gold mines for the trade, but they're real headaches. For awhile I wasn't too sure why we were going to war. I had voted for Woodrow Wilson, (I always voted all the girls, sometimes twice a day, for the ward boss on election day). Wilson, he had "kept us out of the war" and "we were too proud to fight." I didn't feel too badly when the bugles began to play "Over There," and the whores, dressed in white as Red Cross gals, went around in the afternoons to help the Liberty Loan drive. It was good because they'd often bring back some John or high ranking officer or Senator and the girls felt they were doubling the good they were doing.

The stealing in the city government had been going from worse to worse, and the papers were writing us up, which was bad. The City Council, aware of the demand for sexual expression that was swamping the town, took new graft, and established in July 1917 a special section of town for Negro prostitutes, confined from upper Perdido Street to the lower side of Locust. But it was all eye-wash; you couldn't anymore separate the girls, black or white, yellow or pink. Everything that could be used was pressed into patriotic service, you might say, and the demand kept growing and growing as the war went on.

Every man and boy wanted to have one last fling before the real war got him. Every farm boy wanted to have one shot at it in a real house before he went off and maybe was killed. I've noticed it before, the way the idea of war and dying makes a man raunchy, and wanting to have at it as much as he could. It wasn't really pleasure at times but a kind of nervous breakdown that could only be treated with a girl and a set-to. Some were insatiable and wrecked themselves, and some just went on like the barnyard rooster after every hen in sight.

In August 1917, the first sign of the end of the party was hinted at, only we didn't believe for sure it meant what it said. Washington began to regulate prostitution within five miles of army camps and navy stations. Regulations followed regulations. Storyville's days were numbered. The boys, it was decided, could die for their country but not get laid for it.

Chapter 13

Mama don't allow no guitar pickin' around here.
Mama don't allow no guitar pickin' around here.
We don't care what mama don't allow,
Gonna pick that guitar anyhow.
Mama don't allow no guitar pickin' around here.

The Last Night

In August 1917 Secretary of War Newton D. Baker issued a ruling forbidding prostitution within a five mile radius of any Army encampment, and the ruling came from Josephus Daniels, Secretary of the Navy, regarding naval stations. Bascom Johnson of the War and Navy Department visited New Orleans, saw Storyville, and informed the Mayor that orders must be obeyed. The Mayor went to Washington without success. Secretary Daniels said that unless the district was closed by the city it would be closed by the Army and Navy. On October 2, 1917, an ordinance in the City Council abolished Storyville:

Traps.

Permitting the legislative recognition of prostitution as a necessary evil in a seaport the size of New Orleans, our city government has believed that the situation could be administered more easily and satisfactorily by confining it within a prescribed area. Our experience has taught us that the reasons for this are unanswerable, but the Navy Department of the Federal government has decided otherwise.

By midnight of November 12, 1917, it would be unlawful to operate a brothel or assignation or sporting house in New Orleans. Some felt the brothels had been given protection and would be reopened. No dice. In October some fire-insurance companies canceled policies in Storyville. The State Fire Marshal investigated rumors of a plot to burn the whole district. The sporting houses prepared to close.

What had brought about the fall of Storyville besides the snide attitudes of the Army and Navy? For these were merely the facade of a sense of guilt and puritan perversion of the sexual act as seen in our pious creeds. All but the American armed forces provided their soldiers and sailors access to women for sexual reasons. Here the idea that young men in the vigor of their youth could be satisfied with magazines, songs, and soggy doughnuts became a standard philosophy.

Our strange revolt against normal biological need was already imbedded in early Christian writings by saints, sinners, reformed whoremasters and repentent prostitutes and defenders of morals. Saint Augustine could point to himself in his youth as an evil fellow wallowing in the pleasure of the act:

> *And what was it that I delighted in, but to love and be beloved? but I kept not the measure of love, of mind to mind, friendship's bright boundary, but out of the muddy concupiscence of the flesh, and the bubblings of youth, mists fumed up which beclouded and overcast my heart . . . I was tossed about, and wasted, and dissipated, and I boiled over in my fornications.*

Other early writers on the subject were even more deeply outraged against women, but in their heated writing one has a sense of an aphrodisiac flame under their churchly robes:

> *In the woman wantonly adorned to capture souls, the garland upon her head is as a single coal or firebrand of Hell to kindle men with that fire . . . In a single day, by her dancing or her perambulation through the town, she inflames with the fire of her lust perhaps twenty of those who behold her, damning the souls God has created and redeemed at such a cost.*

Even the home was not a proper place for the venal act; to enjoy it seemed against the ideals of the creed, and the man who felt safe in his own marriage, legally, blessed by the church, sporting with his own wife, had a shock coming:

> *It is disgraceful to love another man's wife at all or one's own too much. A wise man ought to love his wife with judgment, not with passion. Let a man govern his voluptuous impulses, and not rush headlong into intercourse . . . He who too ardently loves his own wife is an adulterer.*

The most corrupt branch of the holy service, the Inquisitors, had the worst to say about the sexual monster, woman. That many of them were sodomists and proven rapists of the women in their prisons didn't soften their prose:

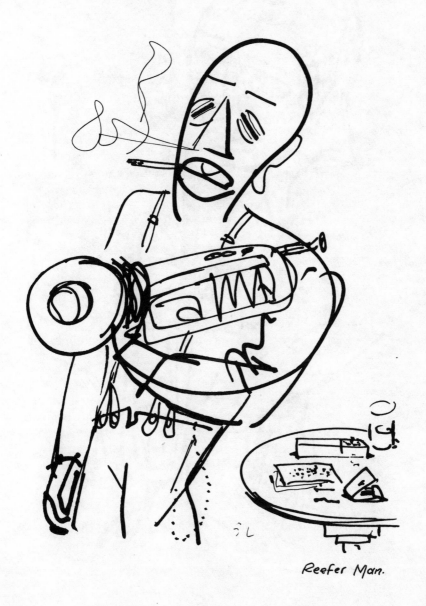

Reefer Man.

Band Break

A woman is beautiful to look upon, contaminating to the touch, and deadly to keep, a foe to friendship, a necessary evil, a natural temptation, a domestic danger, an evil of nature, painted with fair colors, a liar by nature. She seethes with anger and impatience in her whole soul. There is no wrath above the wrath of a woman. Since women are feebler both in mind and body, it is not surprising that they should come under the spell of witchcraft more than men. A woman is more carnal than a man. All witchcraft comes from carnal lust, which is in women insatiable.

This attack on woman as a carnal animal filtered through puritanism. The American strain was always active in matters of morals and the sins of pleasure. Women were the trap, half the *cazzo* and *putta*, the *yoni* and *lingan*, all the tools of the Devil, pronged and cavitied. The human race went to bed and to damnation. The Inquisitors saw woman as the tool of witchcraft and her own foul desires:

These women satisfy their filthy lusts not only in themselves, but even in the mighty ones of the age, of whatever sort and condition, causing by all sorts of witchcraft the death of their souls through the excessive infatuation of carnal love.

All this was to set up the double standard, distort hidden repressions, and, by catering to perverted minds, inflame rapist and pervert, create an underworld of pornography, filthy comic books, under-the-counter trades, whispered vices, blackmail, the badger game, and, of course, divorce rackets which would enrich whole tribes of lawyers.

Storyville in wartime had no chance against all this piled up bile aganst woman's evil, man's fall. A nation proudly at war to "Keep the World Safe for Democracy" could not have its clean boys dominated by their glands and desires when they should be thinking of, perhaps, being honored as the Unknown Soldier. It was more natural to kill your fellow man, than to fornicate.

> *When the revelation comes,*
> *Oh, when the new world is revealed.*
> *Oh, when they gather 'round the throne.*
> *And when they crown Him King of Kings.*
> *And when the sun no more will shine.*
> *And when the moon has turned to blood.*
> *And on that hallelujah day.*
> *When the earth has turned to fire.*
> *When the Saints go marching in.*

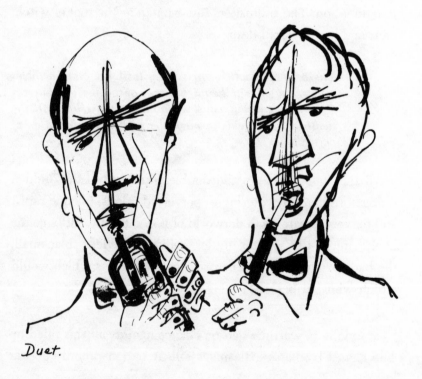

Duet.

One night it was all over. Storyville ended suddenly, like a neck breaking. It meant silence for the Primrose Orchestra, the Magnolia Sweets, Jack Carey's Band and others. The bordello singers didn't believe it. The barrelhouse piano kidded the idea of Storyville as unsanitary and immoral.

Midnight, November 12, came and New Orleans would be a clean town from then on. Sex outside the home would be done away with for good—again. Madame Gertrude Dix tried for a restraining order, but it didn't work. So the wagons were loaded. The crib girls shouldered their mattresses and walked out of Storyville. Beautiful quadroons wept; everyone hung one on. The wet goods flowed. They couldn't move all of it, and the jazz men played new blues for the event.

Nell Kimball wrote of that night:

> I was closing the house with flying colors and I wasn't going on. It was my farewell performance, you might say. For two weeks the wagons and carts had been busy emptying the district. But I had sold the whole shebang, furnishings and all, to a Greek who had opened a quiet little whorehouse near the army base and he would come for the stuff in the morning.
>
> The girls were all in their best evening gowns or rushed negligees, and the old clients and the officers who had become patrons, and the Johns of the sporting and society set that I had been proud of, these I had invited to close my place. I invited fifty people; seventy-five came, acting like they didn't know chalk from cheese. We opened up at nine; we had to close at midnight, put out the old red lantern on the stroke of twelve like some wall-eyed Cinderella.
>
> The girls were all painted and hair piled up, so keyed-up—somebody had been passing a bottle—they sounded

like at a fire. Half of them drunk already, having bribed the nigger maids to get the stuff up from the cellar early. I had sold most of the cellar for ten thousand dollars to the B——Club, for I'd piled up good stuff for years, but I had saved out champagne and brandy and prime aged bourbon and rye. There were hardly any scotch drinkers in those days. I had a keg of lager open in the big parlor and Harry tending bar in the private one. Harry was a bit soaked himself, and he had the big house watchdog, Prince, with him behind the bar nibbling at the buffet where I had the last of the big smoked hams sliced, and the turkey and the fish tidbits and stuff, a whole spread of shrimp gumbos, lobsters and soft shell crabs. It wasn't costing anybody a cent but me—girls, food and drink were on the house. If any of the whores asked for a going away present, well that was up to the John. It didn't matter nohow to me anymore.

About ten o'clock a bunch of hoodlums tried to get in, but the mayor had moved a lot of cops into Storyville that night because there was talk the whores and fancy men were going to burn the place down when they had to leave it. The cops didn't let anybody into my place unless I said they were friends and invited. I didn't want any party crashers or any of the new rich roughnecks in their twenty dollar silk shirts and their rotten manners.

One old gentleman at the party, a judge, he began to cry, sitting on the staircase with two naked whores on his lap, and the professor, the real one, gave a long spiel about Rome falling down, which didn't make much sense to me.

After awhile I got tired of everything and sat in my bedroom with just a few old clients, and they looked old and I felt I was old too. I didn't get drunk as I had expected. The stuff had no bite that night. We just sipped and jawed about girls that were dead, and crazy New Years' and Fourth of Julys, the time we all went to mass and to see a Richmond whore marry a street paving contractor's son, and we talked of the kind of people who were becoming whores these days.

Alice, the society woman from Lake Charles, was mak-

*ing trouble in a gang roll in her room with some of the
army officers. I told Harry to break it up and get her
dressed and into a taxi and headed for the railroad station,
and, I hoped, Lake Charles. She kept pulling off her
clothes as soon as they got them on her and yelling: "Oh,
God, Lake Charles, and Sam, the whole effing thing day
after day! And they call it living." She made crazy talk to
the officers and some of the Johns as to her skill, endurance
and inventing, but Harry got her off in a taxi with a Cajun
girl who was going back to Lafayette where her folks had
a shrimp boat.*

*That was the last real noise in the old place. Midnight
I stood under the big hall chandelier, some of its crystals
gone, and we all had the last drink of flat champagne, the
whores crying, the naked and dressed ones and half-
dressed Johns coming down from upstairs. It was real
sentimental, and I just looked at the ruin of bar and buffet
and the torn cushions and all I could think to do was to
figure out what the night would have brought in if it hadn't
been on the house.*

*But I was through running a sporting house, really
through. I had a bit put away in some stocks that a client
had advised me on. I had a place in Florida where I was
going to live, some lots in St. Louis I had kept the payments up on. I was leaving town and I was handing over
everything with the key-ring to the Greek in the morning.*

*I had been a madame since 1880, and I was feeling stiff
in the joints, and the sporting world wasn't class any more.
The war had changed things and I could see it would
change a lot more, and I didn't want any part of it. I wasn't
tired, and I wasn't involved with any sweet daddy. That
was something I could do without. I always felt a madame
was better off if she was a bit frosty.*

*Some of the madames after Storyville closed tried to
run a secret house, but the police were scared to let them.
There was too much pressure on them. The Department
of Justice had their own men on the scene, and no one
could figure out their price. It wasn't they were honest—
they were unreliable. They raided five places that stayed*

253

The Beat.

open and Gertie Dix got five days in the jailhouse.

Midnight came, and the clients, the Johns passed with it, out of my life. The whores were packed, and hats on the side of their heads, most of them went off with their fancy men. The nigger maids and the handyman went off, toting the remains of the food and a few bottles. Lacy Belle, the cook, was packed, her big blue umbrella rolled under the straps of her leather suitcase, banging the slop pails about when I came into the kitchen to pay her off. She said she was going to Georgia to'stay with relations for a week, then up to Detroit; she didn't want no son of hers—she had two boys at Howard University—to grow up to be called burrheads and get gunned down by the Klan. She was old, too, and her health wasn't too good. I hoped she made it to Detroit and her boys didn't get burned at some Klan barbecue.

That night I slept good and deep for the first time in weeks, and by ten the next morning I said goodbye to Harry and the yard dog, left the keys for the Greek, and was on my way to the railroad station to catch the Florida train. The streets were full of torn paper and broken bottles, and somebody had set an old laundry wagon on fire in Storyville—if it was still Storyville. I loved the goddamn place.

Nell Kimball ended her memoirs here. Unpublished, I acquired them in 1933 when interviewing her in Tampa, Florida. She was then a crinkly old lady with no shred of beauty left. She had been ruined in the Florida land boom of the middle twenties and again in the crash of '29. She had done fairly well as a bootlegger until repeal, and though not rich, was getting by and could see her way clear to live out her years without—she grimaced—going to the poorhouse.

Storyville was closed, but most of the whores and madames merely moved to more respectable parts of town, made their deals with the police, and between raids and payoffs managed to do their business as usual. A comic note was added when some police official said that the unemployed pimps and homosexuals would become patriots and go off to the farms to help raise the crops to beat the Kaiser. There is no indication this ever was taken seriously by those two out-groups.

The hearts of the respectable women of New Orleans ached in pity. Among them the State Federation of Women's Clubs which set up an organization to help the whores. No one came forward as an unemployed harlot to accept this charity. The girls were back at their trade and busier than ever as the war made good times and big spenders. There was a rumor that Madame Dix sent the Federation fifty dollars for whatever use *they* could make of it.

Gin Mill Blues

Storyville's closing increased the illegitimate birthrate. One minister preached about the seduction of girls of good family. More hardened folk like reporters wrote that the daughters of the best families and others were actively engaged in army canteens, bond drives, dances and roadhouse orgies, "giving away what the girls of Storyville had sold." The street walkers were back under the lamplights, the V.D. rate of infection shot up so high the Army and Navy held short arm inspection of all men returning from town, and stations were set up for hygienic aid and advice to men saved from the whorehouses of the French Quarter.

At its flaming height Storyville, according to Chief of Police D. S. Gaster, had 230 sporting houses, 30 houses of assignation, and 2,000 whores. This number kept dropping as moral values changed and the war and the sexual revolution of the Jazz Age shifted all figures.

Chapter 14

Basin Street Blues

With Storyville closed and the new houses illegal, there wasn't use for much music. The Jazz men had to drift north by river, by train, by tin lizzie—the Model T. They went to Memphis, Kansas City, St. Louis, Chicago, east to New York, west to Frisco, spreading the jazz infection.

Jazz had to settle in and grow where it could — in New Orleans and Chicago it got a home. They were both in many ways frontier towns, armed, living with a shrug: "What the hell!" "Live and let live." "Make a buck and have some fun."

258

Imagine jazz being in any town but New Orleans. It had to be a town where the dying was easy, the money came hard, the citizens in love with easy odds and girls, and a new kind of music played by folk you wouldn't care to bring home. Music that put life into a lot of what you feel.

Chicago was a good place. Kansas City, Harlem, bad places. You could live for awhile if you stayed at your trade of making music. But it was cold up north and New Orleans was far away. And the madames had no heart south of the Loop, or up in Harlem.

Most of the up-river pioneers went to Chicago, a city under the thumb of an American folk hero, Al Capone—Little Caesar. His joints used music—lots of it. His sporting houses, road houses, night clubs, all gave work to music makers. He bought the police, the city hall, judges, lawmakers, federal enforcers, reporters; anyone who would take a little, or take big.

Chicago, dirty, fast and with a roar from Dearborn Station to the gold coast lake front, had a flavor of its own. Jazz lived in a special part of the town and it spread its music in a few places. The town along Lake Michigan with a sewer called the Chicago River, the district called the Loop full of El trains, strip tease, burlesque, bump-and-grind. And fashionable shops.

The Negro part of town south of the Loop between the lake and stockyards took in the New Orleans boys. It wasn't as fancy as living on Lake Shore Drive or Detroit's Grosse Point.

Crap Shooter

Slave Song

Night Spot

Moving down State Street from the Loop was the sporting section, the cathouses around 22nd Street, the little dives where they played jazz, shaking from the cold lake breeze blowing through worn down shoes and pants. There were fancy places, too, Pony Moore's, the Everleigh Club. They had piano players, ragtime.

From 1910 they had come here, Bennie Harney, Tony Jackson, Jelly Roll Morton, playing in the houses and at the Elite or Dago and Russell's. Chicago was a tough town. Upright pianos with a kitty to feed. Men like Joe Oliver, Fred Keppard. It was still mostly "nigger music," "whorehouse music." But the music was pleasing and exciting—just as it had been on Basin Street in the French Quarter.

King Oliver sent for Louis Armstrong in New Orleans to take second cornet. Louis was young, strong and eager. He came up from the railroad with his straw suitcase, took up his horn and got in with the band. Louis was good and he and King did duets side by side, hot licks, solid. The King had done well bringing Louis north to play with him.

The Oliver band recorded with Gennett, Paramount, Okeh and Columbia. Nearly thirty-seven sides, the first of great Negro jazz classics of New Orleans cut in wax, "Mabel's Dream," "Canal Street Blues," "Mandy Lee Blues." All favorites.

The Rhythm Kings, white boys, were at the Cascades Ballroom and at Friar Inn. Black-and-white jazz was in Chicago. The whites studied the King and his music—played Dixieland their way and set what was going to influence Chicago style.

The real Chicago School was started early in the '20s. The Wolverines made their first recordings with Bix Biederbecke at cornet. It was good but fuzzy, with no basic beat, only a fast tempo. A little too arranged, and with faked group improvisation. Bix had a beautiful tone, clear, plaintive. New Orleans style was making them see the new ways to play.

Jazz had come a long way from New Orleans. But it was New York that was to change the flow of the original, make it something it wasn't, and make it something that could become a new way of playing. To a lot of people it was the throwing away of the early Negro elements of jazz, in its place a lot of the popular stuff that a white society can accept as music a little more polite than the original forms.

New York changed jazz, not always for the best. Jazz met Tin Pan Alley and pop bands. It couldn't live anymore, lonely on the delta in its sporting house. It had to take on the big town. Jazz took a few steps back, but there were playing cats who kept it pure.

Jazz and Dixieland in New York put up a fight. There were early bands like the Original Hot Five in 1923, and men like Jim Moynahan and his clarinet, Brad Gowans and his trombone. Groups like the Goofus Five, Little Ramblers, California Ramblers and Birmingham Aces, Cotton Pickers, and Ladd's Black Aces. They worked with half-arranged music, a near-crude phrasing. They weren't as wild as Chicago style. The Memphis Five kind of music was being beaten out like the Chicago style. They were more than junk-pile players;

on the move

Field hand Musicians

they had a solid New Orleans Dixieland bass. In its own way it was true to the real jazz. It was full of psycho kick and freakish byplay.

By the middle '20's the *vo-de-o-do* of Bix's Wolverines was was taking over. Loring Red Nichols, one of Bix's followers, was setting a pace for awhile. Arranging was heavy, with the solo featuring the style very close to big band swing.

In the great depression New Orleans-Dixieland-Chicago had become sweet swing. The band firmly on the beat, the syncopation as simple as you can get it. The crooner had gotten into the horns, the trombone became sleek, the reed of the clarinet cloying and sweet, the musical pattern swift and decorative. It was still music and a new way of playing it, but it was housebroken. The flash, the bite, the sporting house phrasing had been replaced by a sentimental accent. Some good men worked in the mood—Artie Shaw, Benny Goodman, the Dorseys, Duke Ellington. It had the face but not the body.

The Mound City Blue Blowers came from St. Louis up river a bit from New Orelans with scat singing and kazoo and banjo, led by Red McKenzie.

> *They laid her out in her cocaine clothes.*
> *She wore a snowbird hat with a crimson rose.*
> *And they wrote on her tombstone this refrain:*
> *She died as she lived, sniffing cocaine.*

Coleman Hawkins had two styles—a slow and fast climbing of scale arpeggios, and a blowing, rising and falling fury. Glenn Miller took the Jack Teagarden and Jimmy Harrison trombone styles and made big loud solos that were only slightly with jazz. The solos in many bands were becoming salon improvisations. They lacked the real New Orleans or Dixieland bite.

There had been jazz in Europe during World War I when the Negro troops brought over their musical feeling. Jim Europe's Band during that war got them used to the brass, and later Louis Armstrong. Europe liked it a lot.

Empty Bed Blues

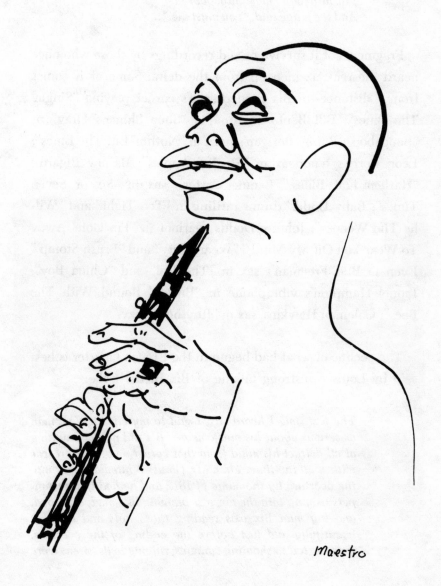

Maestro

You can't hear the sporting house music any more as it had been on Basin Street.

> *They took me to the big jail-house,*
> *The months and months rolled by:*
> *The jury found me guilty, poor boy,*
> *And the judge said, "You must die."*

Fragments of it survive on old recordings by those who once heard the real jazzmen up from the delta. Some of it comes from a distance—in Bix Biederbecke's cornet playing "Singin' The Blues"; Bill Benford's tuba in "Shoe Shiner's Drag" or "Boogaboo"; Bunny Berigan's horn in "Nothin' But The Blues"; Leon Berry's tenor-sax in "Stealin' Apples"; Barney Bigard's "Harlem Flat Blues," Bennie Carter's sax in "Six or Seven Times"; Baby Dodds' drums rattling in "Too Tight" and "Willie The Weeper"; Johnny Dodds' clarinet in "I'm Goin' Away To Wear You Off My Mind," "Weary City" and "Brush Stomp." Even in Bud Freeman's sax in "The Eel" and "China Boy"; Lionel Hampton's vibraphone in "Buzzin' Round With The Bees"; Coleman Hawkins' sax in "Rhythm Crazy."

The decline of what had begun in the French Quarter is best said by Louis Armstrong talking of Bix Biederbecke:

> *The first time I heard Bix, I said to myself: there's a man as serious about his music as me. Bix did not let anything at all detract his mind from that cornet and his heart was with it all the time. Then Mr. (Paul) Whiteman went into the overture by the name of 1812 and he had those trumpets way up into the air, just blowing like mad, but good, and my man Bix was reading those dots and blowing beautifully and just before the ending of the overture, they started to shooting cannons, ringing bells, sirens were*

Singer 1929

Boogie Beat

*howling like mad, and in fact everything was happening
in that overture. But you could still hear Bix.*

You can still hear, if you try, in New Orleans, the old jazz
men's echos as far away now as the ghosts of the sporting
house madams.

Chapter 15

Snakes in the ocean,
Eels in the sea,
Red-headed woman
Made a fool out of me.

When My Baby Says Good Bye

There is no doubt that, as some social historians claim, sexual freedom and the spread of pre-marital fornication with respectable women, destroyed the high standard of the sporting houses for good. By the 1920's, and since, any fairly decent-looking man could get all the unpaid sexual play he wanted without having to go to the professional.

The whorehouse still exists in New Orleans, and every place else in America, but the great days of Liberty Hall are over.

Nobody Knows but Jesus.

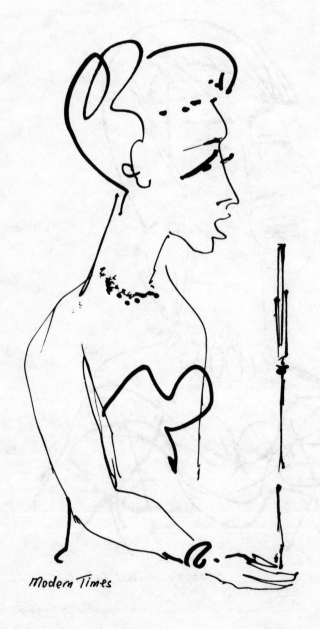

Modern Times

The Mafia and crime syndicates usually control it. The few native American independents are on the outside and don't amount to much. These places exist because the cop and the politician, often right up to the top in Washington are still on the take in one way or another. Smart independent lawyers, so much better than the Federal ones, have kept the government from destroying the syndicate, or deporting too many of its big time gang chiefs who work whores, drugs, gambling, and are now in the hotel business, banking and other legitimate businesses.

In most American cities, as in New Orleans, the call girl, a free lance pleasure pot, only loosely connected to a central office or phone service, has taken over the job of the sporting houses. She is used by big business, international cartels, corporations, fraternal organization, sales conventions. Most of these keep or list call girls.

The call girl is now an American tradition, like Daniel Boone, or the Fourth of July. A recent daily newspaper story links them with the nation's top men and the gentry in Congress. A girl can't do much better than this:

FBI SAYS BAKER CASE FIGURE
HIRED CALL GIRLS

Admitted Obtaining Women to Entertain Customers
Myron (Mickey) Weiner, who paid Bobby Baker $5,000 for "legal fees," admitted he used the services of party girls, according to FBI reports given to the Senate Rules Committee.

A summary of the FBI file was made public Wednesday along with the Senate committee's final report on Baker, former secretary to Senate Democrats.

The summary dealt with activities of Washington call girls.

Weiner, representative of a group of ocean-going freight forwarders, was mentioned on several occasions in the FBI summary. The summary said Weiner "stated he kept the names and telephone numbers of 'a few girls' in the event 'one of his customers' desired female company while in town."

One of the former call girls, identified only as "Mrs. A," admitted "having sexual intercourse with persons in the executive, legislative and judicial branches of government but declined to identify the individuals involved," the FBI report said.

"Mrs. A" also "named four other women, whom she said had engaged in prostitution," according to the report.

Two unnamed employes of a Senate committee, reportedly double-dated.

In his covering letter, Katzenbach said "there is no scintilla of evidence" to indicate the two Senate employes "divulged official matters to call girls or that they compromised their Senate positions in any way."

A woman, designated "Miss C," was said in the FBI summary to have "advised that she had been a party girl. With the exception of one congressman she could identify none of the men she met," the report said.

Another woman, "Miss E," admitted "prostitution activities at the behest of Mrs. A," who had told investigators "she might be termed a 'madam.'"

Call girls, well dressed, over-combed, blase, bored, often mental cases, exist in good apartments, contact their work through phone exchanges. Their prices are high; a hundred dollars a trick, as a sexual encounter is called, is the accepted fee. Specialists providing for the demands of the jaded and perverted call for extra payment. The girls drive Cadillacs, own French poodles, are often alcoholics, drug addicts and some-

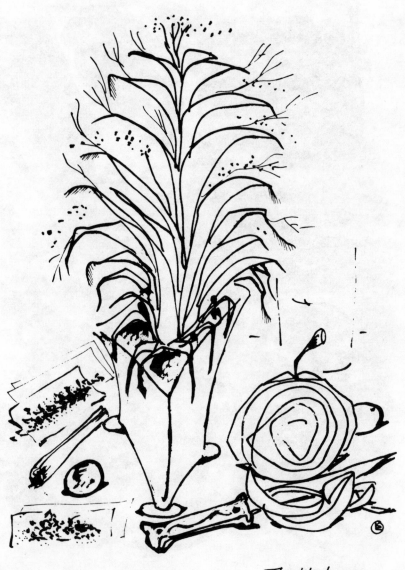

The Weed

Showboat Jazz.

times are on the Freudian couch as well as on the Beautyrest.

In New Orleans they are on housecall at most hotels, either through the bell captain or some desk man. They are on parade at the better places in stretch pants, at the pools in bikinis. Many work out of the motels that ring the city, at the tourists' rests and even in the trailer camps. They are not the girls of Storyville, plump, feminine, over-curved and costumed in flared negligee to attract the male eye of the period. The modern call girl is slim, boyish in an age of Momism and homsexuality, better educated, often well read. But a social misfit, neurotic, and given to talk of suicide and death.

The demand is greater than ever. One private sociological source report states:

> Because of the community property laws and high cost of divorce, many men prefer call girls to getting married. Men who have been married one or two times also feel a sense of escape, free of domestic burdens they do not want to take on again. While sexual intercourse has come a long way since the single standard. There are, with non-whores, risks on pregnancies, pressure to marry, sleeping with a prostitute avoids all this in our hurrying society.
>
> Extra-marital adventures are almost the pattern in most divisions of our society. In the theatrical world, industry, big business, advertising, the call girl is nearly a respected status symbol. To have bedded some famous New York fashion model, or a girl who once had a fleeting moment of fame in motion pictures, sets up an individual (in certain fields) as a man of the world.
>
> The bed life of upper middle class people is definitely less loyal than it has been. The bored women have more time for shopping, games, club work, and the home has lost its center as the core of a modern marriage. Jet flights,

the rush to travel abroad, the wearing pressure of the pecking order of corporation life with its social patterns, where a company wife can make or break a man, all these lead to promiscuity on a broader casual plane.

The idea of sin is nearly gone and the breakdown of faith in an Old Testament God and his punishing Hebrew way, the lack of belief in a large part of the population in a real Hell and Heaven, all these things have geared men and women today to a wilder search for sexual satisfaction away from the home.

The erotic revolution among the young, where fornication even among highschool students is often accepted as the normal pattern in our baffled age, increased the national sexual expression. The publication of Playboy-type magazines with their huge fold-out full-colored photographs of nude girls breaks down the last mystery. The puritan safeguards of guilt and moral restraint, while not fully displaced, are pushed aside when unmarried copulation is no longer the social and character-destroying act it was considered in pre-World War I times and later.

The sexual revolution has not made Americans any happier. It has merely given them more problems to face and caused them, under new tensions, to seek release in the very thing that was causing the tensions to begin with. In such an atmosphere the B-girl who works the bars and the call girl who waits by her phone and the half amateur street walker are still with us and will continue to be.

For all the Kinsey research, sex manuals to happiness, beatnik morals, women's magazines rehashing of once blushing clinical facts, our sexual patterns and mores still have wrinkles in them.

And what of the sporting house jazz men. Every day the papers record one more passing:

FIRST IMPRESARIO OF QUARTER DIES.
They buried Jack Robertson today.
A few friends did. There were no relatives, just a few friends. There were only a few because, at 84, Jack Robert-

Man with a Horn.

Buddy Bolden Blues.

son had outlived most of his old friends. Friends like "Stale Bread" Charlie Lacomb, who scraped a cigar box fiddle. And "Warm Gravy." And drummer Charley Stein. And "Whiskey" Benrod and Frank "Monk" Bussey and "Chinee," the bull fiddle player. All members of the "Razzy Dazzy Spasm Band." And Julia Dean, Nina Jackson, Jessie Brown and Antonia Gonzales — whose establishments sometimes echoed to the ragtime of the Razzy Dazzy band. And who were just as popular.

And Sarah Bernhardt, "Divine Sarah," who once visited Jack shortly after he went into business. Jack Robertson's friends were many and varied — the madcaps and madames, the queens and characters of the old French Quarter. But this figures because Jack Robertson opened and operated the first cabaret in the French Quarter: The Haymarket on Customhouse Street between Dauphine and Bourbon. The date was 1911. (Customhouse Street is now Iberville and the site of the old Haymarket is now occupied by the warehouse of D. H. Holmes Co. Ltd.)

Jack Robertson lived "high off the hog," according to Harry Gregson, retired police captain who was the organizer and singer of the Razzy Dazzy Jazz Band. "He lived hard. Drank hard. But he was the softest touch in the Quarter. If he didn't gamble his money away, he gave it away."

Jack Robertson died "straight and proud. He carried himself like a soldier." This from Joe Lenfant on the lake front at East End. Robertson had lived with Lenfant for the last 17 years. "He was the finest old man I've ever known. He had more character and strength than anybody half his age. He sold peanuts on the lake front up until a few years ago. Said he wanted to earn his way. He died happy. He said he lived a full life. And had no regrets."

The full life of Jack Robertson started in New Orleans in the early 1900s. When he opened his famous Haymarket cabaret he said: "I brought that name 'cabaret' from New York along with a girl, five snakes and $55. New Orleans went crazy over the snakes. But I ran a good place. The legislators would make laws in Baton Rouge, then come to my place and break them. They broke the fiddles, too. They practiced their speeches in my place. And one big

Below New Orleans.

shot broke a tooth trying to bite the cap off a bottle of beer. I been married but divorced. I still love Mae Evans. You never heard of Mae? She ran a business below Canal. And she was a beauty. She paid me alimony for three years. But she got it all back."

After his Spasm Band left the Haymarket, Robertson hired a group of adult musicians to take their place, calling themselves the Razzy Dazzy Spasm Band. Gregson explains: "The Spasm kids got big rocks and all the rotton fruit we could find and we marched over to the Haymarket. We told Robertson to either 'change them guys' name, or we'd let him have it.' He laughed. And we started throwing. Finally he agreed. And he made them guys call themselves the Razzy Dazzy Jazzy Band. We played for Sarah Bernhardt once. I remember she gave each of us a dime. She came down here to do a big play. At the opera house on Canal."

Gregson paid Robertson the highest honor. "Even the underworld went for the guy. He played it big. But he played it straight."

And this morning a dedicated group of friends followed Jack Robertson to his last resting place.

There is no mention in the press clipping if they played the *real* music at the grave.

Where Storyville once spread itself is now a kind of fairground of a few good eating places and a lot of poor ones, antiques of unproved history, the remains of courtyards made over into tearooms, iron railing kept in good repair. On Bourbon Street the sons and grandchildren of the original jazz men often sit on raised platforms and play the old solid music as it once sounded here above the laughter of promiscuity and the polite hiss of rubber-tired carriages carrying the gentry towards their favorite spot. The present French Quarter is full of cleaned-up history, the old streets have been given back their names. Basin Street is Basin Street again. The humid heat is the same, the river smells just a little worse, and is a little more polluted from industry and progress. The sailing ships are gone, but the delta remains, muddier, still cutting new channels, rushing the silt of a dozen states into the gulf.

The faces on Dauphine, Canal, and Customhouse streets carry memories of the genes of the *metisse, negrillonn,* the thrill hunters, the music makers, the girls and the sports that were here once and are now gone. The dress is different, the fashion is changed. Gone are the goldheaded canes, the wasp-waisted corsets, the top hat, the wing collar; even the spats are lost and the derbys, and butter-gold watch chains heavy across a waistcoat on a well-fed paunch. Missing for good are the smell of the horse, and the horse himself. But from the river comes the odor of coffee in bags and tropical fruit tang reaches the last houses that remember wild nights, great lovings along these streets. Most of the houses once carried red latterns and the music came from behind drawn plush velvet drapes and closed shutters.

The great madames are only obscure items in yellowing newspaper files. Kate Townsend, Fanny Sweet, Red Light Liz (the love of Joe the Whipper), Nelly Gasper, Fanny Peel. And the cribhouse bawds with the strange names: Kidney Foot Jenny, One Eye Sal, Gallus Lu, Fighting Mary, who were all the pride of Smoky Row between Bienville and Conti Streets, are long buried.

Memory is vague among the town's historians about Spanish Agnes, Miss Carol, the limpwristed homosexuals called

Waiting

Lady Beulah, Chicago Belle and Lady Richard. There have been other changes. The Negro has come out of the shadow and demands to be counted a human being. The old Southern families have died out or been absorbed by the shanty boat hands, the rednecks and the poor white trash grown rich on oil and lumber and cotton and war and government contracts.

The Confederate flag has been disgraced and become a badge of biggots and assassins.No one talks much any more about how fine it was in the old days "befoh de wah." That war is a century away and getting as dim as the voices with nearly forgotten words.

> *Did you ever hear about Cocaine Lil?*
> *She lived in a house on a cocaine hill.*
> *She had a cocaine dog and a cocaine cat.*
> *They fought all night with a cocaine rat.*
>
> *She had cocaine hair on her cocaine head.*
> *She had a cocaine dress that was poppy red.*
> *But the cocaine blues, they made her sad.*
> *Oh, the cocaine blues, they made her feel bad.*

The champagne and bourbon have been replaced by Hadacol-and-cola. The young hell-raisers don't push over backyard privies, but smoke pot and ride Hondas and to them all of the past is square.

And the sporting house girls? Nobody remembers many of their names. They came to town, they did their business, they died, or moved on carrying their belongings in a straw suitcase, their frowsy skirts dragging on the slate sidewalks. Mostly not too sober, not too bright. But with good legs, and breasts

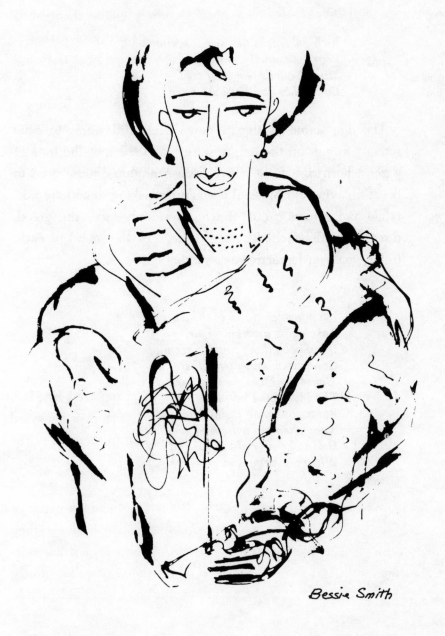

Bessie Smith

round and smooth as an egg. They weren't very practical, had no hearts of gold, and they never had much luck or glamor out of bed.

> Rich gal smells like sweet perfume.
> Poor gal's smell is a shame.
> My gal smells like billy goat —
> But it's her smell just the same.

The dim sound of the rundown heels still seems to echo some mornings on the empty streets, and the metallic tone of a ghost horn rises from where Josie Arlington's house used to be. It's playing old blues. But you'd be making something nostalgic and romantic out of what was only vice, sin, greed, disease and debauched lives, if instead of the sound of early traffic, you heard a reedy voice singing:

> I'm gonna go down to the levee,
> Take along a rockin' chair.
> If my baby don't come to see me,
> Gonna rock away from there.
> 'Cause the blues ain't nothin'
> The blues ain't nothin'
> But a good man feelin' bad.
> Now when my baby said goodbye,
> Had to break right down and cry,
> When my baby said goodbye.

Good Bye